For Elmer Rowley

With my very best

wishes.

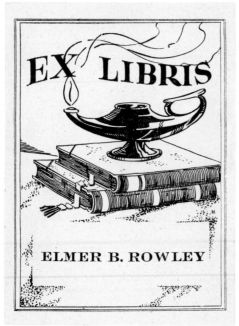

EX LIBRIS

ELMER B. ROWLEY

Bob Gait.

June, 1975.

Exploring Minerals & Crystals

General Editor —
Peter C. Swann, M.A. (Oxon.),
LL.D. (Brock)
Director, The Royal Ontario Museum

Exploring Minerals & Crystals

Robert I. Gait

Associate Curator
Department of Mineralogy
Royal Ontario Museum

Photographs by ARTHUR WILLIAMS

McGRAW-HILL RYERSON LIMITED

Toronto   Montreal   New York   London   Sydney   Mexico
Johannesburg   Panama   Düsseldorf   Singapore   Rio de Janeiro
Kuala Lumpur   New Delhi

Preface

This book attempts to answer the apparently simple, yet rather difficult question: What is a mineral? Probably it will raise more questions than it answers; but I hope the reader will be tempted to ask himself some and then set out in search of the answers.

To Dr. Peter Swann, Director of the Royal Ontario Museum, Toronto, I would like to express my gratitude, not only for his invitation to write this book, but also for his strong encouragement, help and support throughout its evolution. The Royal Ontario Museum kindly made available materials from its galleries and collections for the illustrations; without this *Exploring Minerals and Crystals* could not have been written. I would like to thank Dr. J. A. Mandarino, Curator of Mineralogy at the Royal Ontario Museum, for his critical reading of the manuscript; his comments and suggestions greatly improved the final version. Mr. Arthur B. F. Williams, Assistant Photographer at the Royal Ontario Museum, took all the photographs; for his painstaking work, I offer my sincere gratitude. Miss Muriel Ward typed the manuscript and I thank her for a job well done. Many friends and associates deserve thanks for their advice and helpful suggestions.

R. I. G.

Contents

An Introduction   9

Colour Plates 1-15   17

Atoms and Crystals   27

More About Crystals   37

The Growth of Crystals   51

The Physical Properties
of Minerals —1   61

The Physical Properties
of Minerals — 2   69

Colour Plates 16-38   81

Non-Silicate Minerals:
A Classification   91

Silicate Minerals:
A Classification   103

Some References   117

Index   118

An Introduction

At some time or another everyone has picked up a mineral and perhaps wondered about it. Everyone has some idea of what a mineral is, but for the time being we shall simply say that a mineral is any material which is not produced by living things. Or we could say a mineral is formed by natural processes which have not been directly affected by living things.

There are many ways of studying minerals, all of them fascinating, which range from a simple descriptive approach to a highly sophisticated scientific study. For us to understand minerals, these kinds of study must be made together; neither makes sense without the other.

We are fascinated by the natural minerals around us because they are part of our environment and help us to understand our place in nature. Minerals are an important part of this environment and are particularly attractive because of their wonderful crystal shapes, forms and colours. Minerals are not only beautiful; their crystals have a symmetry which immediately makes one wonder how nature could have formed them so unvaryingly.

Minerals make up the rocks of the crust of the earth and probably the interior of this planet on which we live. From minerals we obtain the raw materials (gold, copper, iron, diamonds, etc.) necessary for our technology and therefore geologists go to great lengths to study rock formations to find those which are most likely to contain valuable minerals (Figs. 1-1, 1-2).

Scientists study minerals because they illustrate nature's ways of combining elements into compounds and crystal structures; their interests lie mainly in the chemistry and physics of minerals. Gemmologists study minerals to determine whether they can be cut into pleasing gemstones: this depends upon their colour, brilliance, hardness,

Published by courtesy of Aluminum Company of Canada Ltd.

Fig. 1-1 Molten aluminum at temperatures between 1250-1350°F (670-720°C) is poured from a holding furnace into moulds of required ingot shape.

Fig. 1-2 An aerial view of Alcan's Arvida works in the Saguenay district of Quebec. This the largest aluminum smelter in the world. It is located here because of abundant hydro-electric power and nearby deep-sea port facilities. The raw material, bauxite, is brought by sea from South America

rarity and beauty. Mining companies are interested in minerals containing useful elements which are profitable to mine. Miners study minerals to learn how they react to mining processes—drilling, breaking and blasting. Even prehistoric man had an interest in rocks and minerals. He sought those which possessed the best properties for making cutting and stabbing instruments (Fig. 1-3), as well as those which had suitable colours for making the paints with which he could draw himself and the animals in his world.

Many people collect minerals because they exhibit lovely colours, striking crystals or fascinating patterns. This is a form of collecting in which everybody, young or old, rich or poor, can share. Museum collections usually display the more colourful and spectacular minerals for the enjoyment of the public. This serves a two-fold purpose: first, it interests young people in the science of mineralogy, and encourages them to become mineralogists or geologists; secondly, it gives us an opportunity to see the wonders of nature, their infinite variety, and in general to appreciate the world in which we live.

Anybody interested in learning about minerals can do so easily. Anyone can collect them without much difficulty by joining an amateur mineral group and participating in a field trip to a mine dump or quarry where good mineral specimens can be picked up. To identify the

Published by courtesy of Aluminum Company of Canada Ltd.

Fig. 1-3   From earliest times man has dug in the ground for materials for tools and weapons. This is an ancient arrowhead from the Rainy River district of Ontario. Specimen courtesy of Dr. Walter Kenyon

minerals he finds, some experience and study are necessary; and, like anything else, the more information he gets about the specimens in his collection, the more interesting and valuable the collection becomes.

The trained mineralogist has made a thorough study of geology, chemistry, physics and mathematics to fit him for his profession; some physicists and chemists devote much of their time to the study of minerals. Indeed minerals themselves led to the development of some of the scientific disciplines: chemistry developed from attempts to extract the valuable elements contained in minerals, and crystallography, the study of crystals, developed from the desire to describe the shapes of natural crystals. Few branches of study can be treated from so many levels, and certainly few sciences so pleasingly combine exact knowledge with sheer beauty.

Research in mineralogy is conducted in many institutions, universities and museums throughout the world, and it is becoming increasingly apparent that such studies lead to significant contributions to our modern way of life. Mineralogy is just one aspect of geology, but it is one which is comparatively concise and precise in terms of the chemistry and physics involved. So let us look at some of the fields of geology, or earth science, described briefly below:

Mineralogy: the study of minerals, the materials which form all rocks, and hence the earth, and probably the universe itself.

Petrology: the study of the ways in which minerals occur together to form rocks, and the study of the rocks themselves.

Economic Geology: the study of the occurrence and formation of minerals which are of sufficient value and in great enough quantities to be mined economically.

Geophysics: the study of the overall structure of the earth and the universe.

Palaeontology: the study of very ancient life by the description and study of fossil animals and plants.

Stratigraphy: the study of the history of the crust of the earth as revealed by the layering of the rocks and the fossils contained in them.

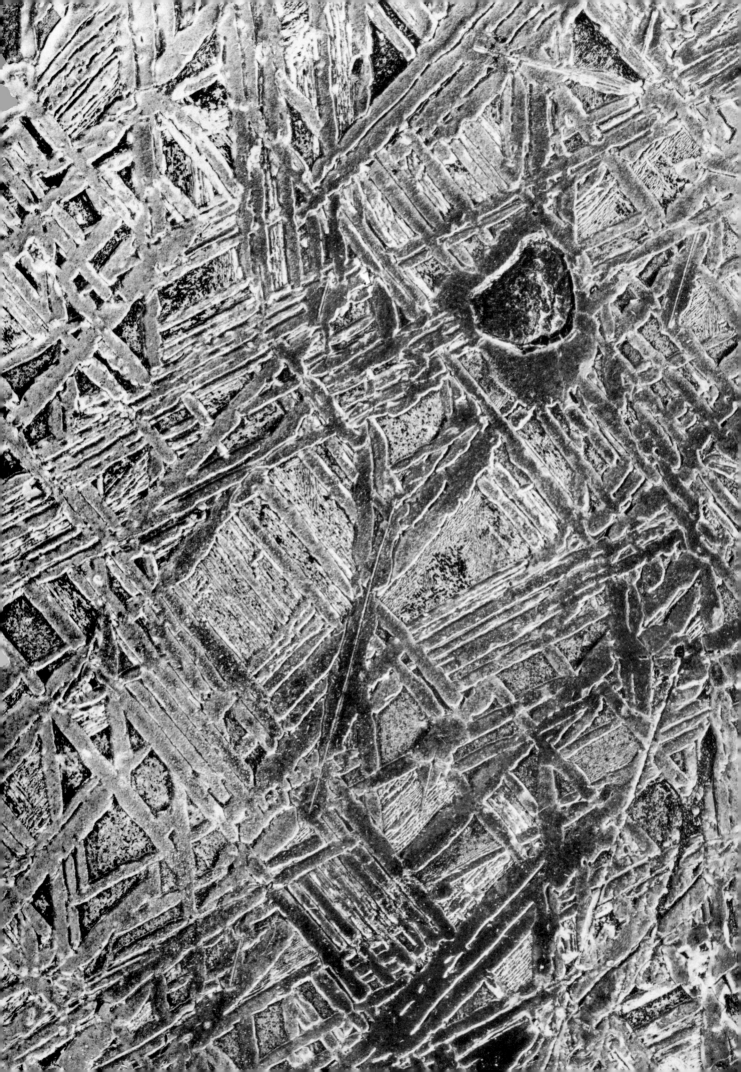

The above list mentions only some of the divisions of earth science, there are many others. Do not forget that the principles of these subjects may apply equally well to the other heavenly bodies such as the moon and other planets. In fact geology has long been involved with astronomy and has produced theories to account for the origin of the earth, the moon, the solar system and the universe in general. Mineralogists have studied the minerals in meteorites (Fig. 1-4), and currently are examining the minerals in the rocks from the surface of the moon. They will also learn about the minerals from the other heavenly bodies when these become available.

Just as geology has various divisions, mineralogy also can be divided into several subjects. The main ones are:

Morphological crystallography, the study of the outward appearance and shapes of crystals.

Structural crystallography, the study of the arrangements of atoms within crystals.

Crystal chemistry or *chemical crystallography*, the study of the kinds of atoms present in a mineral, their arrangements and the ways in which they are related to the properties of the mineral.

Optical crystallography, the study of the optical character of minerals.

Physical mineralogy, the study of the physical properties of minerals, which include lustre, colour, hardness, electrical, magnetic and several other properties.

As we have seen, mineralogy dates from prehistory, when primitive man learned to use various rocks and minerals for making tools, and to use certain powdered minerals as colouring material for paints. In historical times mineral studies have progressed from peculiar legends to the firm scientific basis upon which the subject now stands.

Alas, a mineral is almost impossible to define since there are exceptions to any of the definitions so far proposed. The simplest and most commonly used definition is:

A MINERAL IS A NATURALLY OCCURRING INORGANIC ELEMENT OR COMPOUND.

Naturally occurring means that the mineral is formed by nature and is not man-made.

Fig. 1-4   The etched surface of this meteorite reveals the interlocking pattern of crystals. The specimen is about 7 x 5 cm. and comes from Augusta County, Virginia, U.S.A.

13

Inorganic elements or compounds are those materials which are formed without the direct action of living things.

An *element* is a material composed of only one kind of atom. Gold is made entirely of gold atoms and copper is made entirely of copper atoms.

A *compound* is a material made of two or more kinds of atoms. Thus halite (common salt) is a compound since it contains atoms of sodium and atoms of chlorine. Compounds contain definite amounts of the various kinds of atoms which form them. In salt the number of sodium and chlorine atoms is equal.

This definition has drawbacks, as well as advantages and is satisfactory only in general terms. Some minerals are not inorganic but are composed of organic compounds which were formed, however, without the direct action of living organisms. This latter statement is important and our definition could be rewritten as follows:
A MINERAL IS A NATURALLY OCCURRING ELEMENT OR COMPOUND, THE FORMATION OF WHICH DOES NOT INVOLVE THE ACTION OF A LIVING ORGANISM.

Many natural materials appear as if they ought to be classified as minerals and yet are not. Pearls are non-mineral since they are formed by the action of a shellfish in its attempt to soothe the irritation caused by a fragment of foreign material, such as a grain of sand. Crystals grown in the laboratory are not minerals since they are not formed by nature. Even synthetic materials which are chemically and physically identical to minerals are not considered as such. Some other examples of non-minerals are coral, bone, amber (the fossil resin of trees) and ivory, which were formed by living things.

In general, minerals are solid materials although water and mercury also are considered as minerals.

Since our definition states that minerals are naturally occurring elements or compounds, and these have definite chemical compositions, it follows that minerals also must have definite chemical compositions. This, in turn, means that the proportions of the atoms in the mineral must be constant. Thus a mineral like galena (Fig. 1-5), composed of lead and sulphur atoms, has a definite proportion of lead to sulphur. For every atom of lead in galena there is one of sulphur, so the proportions

Fig. 1-5   A fine octahedral crystal of galena about 3½ cm. on an edge. The specimen comes from Baxter Springs, Kansas, U.S.A.

14

are equal. The chemical composition can be written simply as PbS using the standard chemical symbols— lead (Pb), sulphur (S). But although this definite proportion is ideally required by the definition, many minerals are found which show variations in their chemical compositions. The variation, however, can only be within certain limits, otherwise the nature of the material will be changed appreciably; and if the amounts of the impurities are great, the material may be changed enough to be classified as a different mineral with a different composition from the ideal.

Most minerals are crystalline and many are found as regularly formed shapes (crystals). Crystals are made up of definite and regular arrangements of atoms. It is these arrangements, together with the kinds of elements (atoms) present, which are responsible for the properties of minerals. An understanding of the meaning of crystallinity is one of the basic aspects of mineralogy.

In this book the emphasis will be on the kinds and arrangements of atoms in minerals and their effects upon the various physical properties by which minerals can be described. This will make it possible for the reader to understand the physical properties of minerals.

This approach should answer such questions as why graphite is soft and black, while a diamond is hard and usually transparent, although both are made of the same kinds of atoms; why certain minerals are heavier than others; why minerals of the Mica Group always occur as flat sheets, piled together like the leaves of a book; why some minerals are coloured and others are not, and why some are radioactive.

1

Plate 1   The arrangement of lead (black) and
sulphur (yellow) atoms in galena. A specimen of
galena is on the right

2 3

4

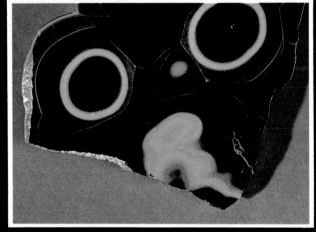

5

Plate 2   Crystals of galena, mainly cubes but octahedral faces may be seen at the corners of the cubes (see drawing, Fig. 2-9). Largest crystal is 1 cm. across. Japan

Plate 3   Twinned crystals of dolomite about 3 cm. high. Spain

Plate 4   Scolecite: a radiating group of crystals about 6 cm. long. Iceland

Plate 5   Malachite: a polished slab about 10 cm. long. Katanga, Republic of the Congo

Plate 6   Muscovite crystals. Brazil

Plate 7   Petrified wood. The wood has been
replaced by opal. 25 x 19 cm. Idaho, U.S.A.

Plate 8   A phantom quartz crystal. 13 x 5 cm.

Plate 9   A partial phantom calcite crystal from
Mexico

Plate 10   Phantom calcite (two views). The milky-
white calcite is coated with copper crystals and
then overgrown with clear calcite. Michigan,
U.S.A.

Plate 11   Chalcopyrite crystals (brassy) in
parallel growth on sphalerite (dark brown)

12 a

12 b

Plate 12 A group of barite crystals. (a) This view
shows a predominance of red hematite. (b) The
same specimen from another angle showing less
hematite. England

13

14

15

Plate 13   Quartz: colour and pattern varieties used as gemstones and ornaments. Royal Ontario Museum display

Plate 14   Uraninite (top, left) and fluorite (top, right). The arrangements of atoms in each mineral are the same. Uraninite model (bottom, left): silver atoms — uranium, red atoms — oxygen. Fluorite model (bottom, right): orange atoms — calcium, clear atoms — fluorine

Plate 15   Kyanite: softest parallel to the blade, hardest across the blade.   Kenya

Atoms and Crystals

We have mentioned already that atoms make up all materials we know. It is important therefore for us to understand atoms and how they make crystals and non-crystals. Since minerals are mainly crystalline materials, we shall pay special attention to the concepts of crystallography, to discover how atoms may be arranged in a regular way to make crystals.

Atoms

Let us get down to a few fundamentals. Chemists and physicists like to refer to all things as *matter*. More familiar words are materials or substances. Everything we know—rocks, desks, plants, air—is made of atoms, which are the fundamental parts of all elements. Elements are made of only one kind of atom; thus gold is made of gold atoms, copper of copper atoms, lead of lead atoms, and so on. Even a tiny microscopic piece of an element contains millions of atoms. There are 105 basic kinds of atoms known and so there are only 105 different elements. In theory, it is possible to break an element into smaller and smaller pieces, taking away atoms, until all that is left is one atom. This remaining atom still represents the chemical nature of the element but if we make this atom smaller by removing portions of it, it will no longer represent the chemical nature of the element of which it was a part. *An atom therefore is the smallest part of an element which is chemically characteristic of that element.* In most mineral studies, atoms are the smallest particles which enter into the description of minerals.

Atoms generally may be thought of as very small spheres. Each of the 105 basic atoms possesses its own characteristic size, weight and chemical nature. An atom of average size is about $1/100,000,000$ (one/one hundred millionths) of a centimetre in radius—there are about $2\frac{1}{2}$ centimetres to an

Scale: 1/2,000,000 of a centimetre

Fig. 2-1 A row of 25 atoms. Each atom is 1/100,000,000 of a centimetre in radius

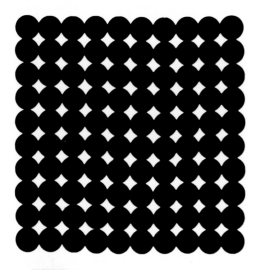

1 square centimetre

Fig. 2-2 Rows of atoms regularly arranged to make a plane

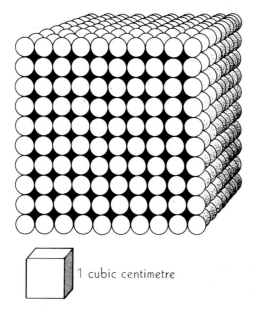
1 cubic centimetre

Fig. 2-3 A three-dimensional arrangement of atoms. Note their regularity

inch—and in diameter this atom would be 2/100,000,000 (two/one hundredth millionths) of a centimetre. Thus, if atoms of this size could be lined up in a single row, there would be fifty million atoms in every centimetre along the row (Fig. 2-1). Most elements are crystalline and have their atoms arranged in a regular manner.

Fig. 2-1 shows a straight row of atoms; if we were to join together many such rows by placing them alongside each other in a regular manner, we could produce a regular layer of atoms; and every square centimetre of the layer would contain 2,500,000,000,000,000 atoms or two thousand five hundred million million atoms. Fig. 2-2 shows a layer of atoms like this and its regular arrangement is obvious, but it has only two dimensions. Now we have to add to it in the third dimension, so we can pile many layers of atoms one on another. Because we are following the rules of crystallinity, we can use only identical layers and they must be piled in a regular manner. This is shown in Fig. 2-3; a cubic centimetre of this arrangement will contain about 125,000,000,000,000,000,000,000, or one hundred and twenty-five thousand million million million atoms.

It is difficult of course to deal with such numbers and fractions to describe the sizes and numbers of atoms, so scientists use what is called the Ångstrom unit which is equal to 1/100,000,000 of a centimetre (usually written as 1×10^{-8} cms.). The radius of our atom which we used to make the three-dimensional arrangement is therefore 1 Ångstrom unit, and its diameter is 2 Ångstrom units. The word Ångstrom can be abbreviated to Å.

But atoms vary in size. Some familiar elements— gold, silver, copper, iron, silicon and aluminum— are made of atoms which are smaller than 1 Å in radius. Other elements, such as sulphur, fluorine, calcium, strontium and potassium, are made of

28

Fig. 2-4   The arrangement of atoms in the crystal structure of lead

atoms which are larger than 1 Å. Imagine the number of atoms in a bar of copper from a smelter, weighing perhaps one hundred pounds!

The illustration 2-4 shows part of a model of the arrangement of lead atoms as they would be in a piece of lead. Careful study of the picture will show that the atoms are arranged in rows, the rows are arranged to make layers, and the layers piled regularly together make up the regular three-dimensional arrangement. Notice that, although the model looks irregular, the arrangement of atoms is the same throughout. On one part of the model the atoms make a shape which is completed on all sides by smooth planes of atoms. These planes are parallel to the other distinct planes of atoms. This shape corresponds to a possible crystal of lead, since it is the prominent planes of atoms in an arrangement which are most likely to form the crystal faces.

Some elements can be mixed together without anything happening; for example, we could place lumps of sulphur and lumps of lead on a dish. It remains a simple mixture. With tweezers, or by hand, it is possible to separate the different elements. This is called a physical mixture. The amounts of sulphur and lead in the mixture may be varied without altering the fact that it is still a mixture and the two elements can be separated easily. If, however, a chemical reaction occurs between the lead and sulphur, perhaps stimulated by heating in a furnace, a chemical compound is formed. Let us look at Plate 1 (page 17), which shows a model of the arrangement of atoms in such a compound. The regular arrangement is defined by the rows and layers of atoms; lead atoms are the small black spheres, and sulphur is represented by the large yellow spheres. Notice that each atom is closely connected with each other atom and that every lead atom has a sulphur atom next to it. If we were to count the numbers of lead atoms and sulphur atoms in this three-dimensional model, we would find that there are very nearly the same number of each kind. This means that, for this particular compound, there is one atom of lead for every atom of sulphur. Since the chemical symbols for lead and sulphur are Pb and S, the

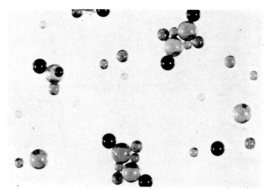

Fig. 2-5a   The arrangement of atoms in a non-crystalline material

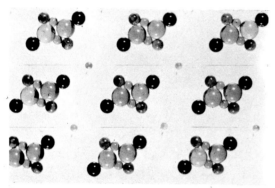

Fig. 2-5b   The regular arrangement of atoms in a crystalline material

Fig. 2-6   Four views of the same model representing a simple cubic repeat pattern:
(a) A general view
(b) A special view from the centre of one face to the centre of the opposite face. Note the four-fold symmetry
(c) Another special view from one corner diagonally through the body centre to the opposite corner. Note the three-fold symmetry

composition of the compound can be written Pb_1S_1, but the 1s usually are taken for granted and it is written simply PbS. The same picture (Plate 1) shows a specimen of the mineral galena; its composition is PbS, and the arrangement of atoms in this crystalline mineral is the one we have been talking about.

Other chemical compounds may have different amounts of atoms in them; the mineral pyrite has two atoms of sulphur for every atom of iron. Its chemical composition therefore can be written FeS_2 (Fe is the chemical symbol for iron). It is a natural crystalline material and therefore possesses a regular arrangement of atoms.

So there are two main kinds of regular arrangements of atoms: those which consist of only one kind of atom (the chemical elements), and those which may contain two or more different kinds of atoms (the chemical compounds). Minerals can be either one; gold is a native element, pyrite is a natural chemical compound. Both are minerals. Both have a definite chemical composition that varies only slightly from the ideal.

The Building Blocks of Crystals

Crystals are those materials which are characterized by regular arrangements of atoms. Non-crystalline materials have their atoms scattered around and not specially arranged. The photograph (Fig. 2-5a and b) shows two models illustrating this difference. We must remember, too, that materials (both crystals and non-crystals) are made up of three-dimensional arrangements. Fig. 2-6 shows a three-dimensional regular arrangement of atoms.

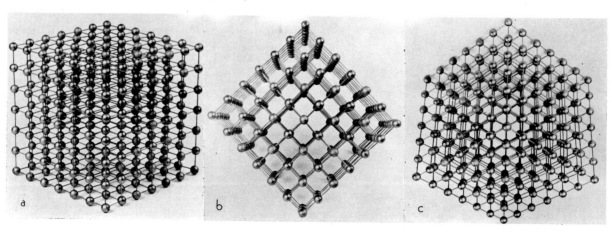

The regular arrangement is obvious and, since the atoms are all of the same kind, this model represents one of the possible arrangements of atoms in an element. The atoms have been separated from each other by short rods to make it easier to see the orderly arrangement, since in most crystals the atoms actually touch one another. The arrangement of atoms in Fig. 2-6 is the same as that which we built in Figs. 2-1, -2, and -3.

If we look at Fig. 2-6, we can easily see that the whole arrangement is made up of repeating cube-shaped units. This is one of the six basic shapes of the building blocks of crystals. All minerals which are said to belong in the cubic system in crystallography have arrangements of atoms which can be described by a cubic repeat pattern which is basically the same as the one shown here.

The cube and the other five building-block shapes are shown in Fig. 2-7. Each one can be made by starting with rows of atoms and then making planes using the rows, but offsetting the rows in a regular way. These planes then can be

Fig. 2-7   The six basic building blocks of crystals

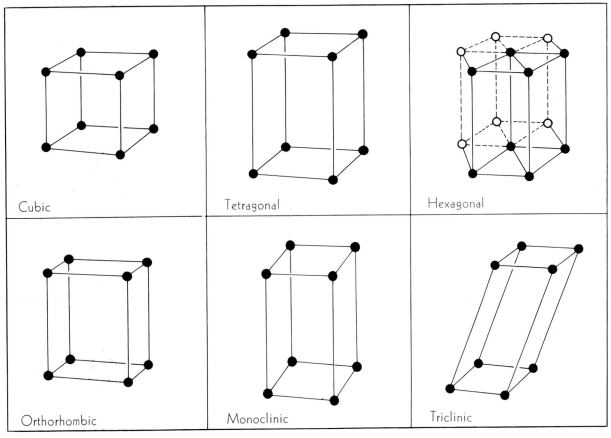

Cubic

Tetragonal

Hexagonal

Orthorhombic

Monoclinic

Triclinic

used to build the three-dimensional arrangements, and these also can be offset in a regular manner. The only rule to remember when doing this is that the arrangements must be regular, so that the repetition from one atom to the next is constant throughout the whole structure. If we follow this rule, only six different three-dimensional patterns can be made and these correspond to the six basic building blocks of all crystals. Each shape is given a name: *cubic* (properly called *isometric*), *tetragonal*, *hexagonal*, *orthorhombic*, *monoclinic* and *triclinic*, which are also the names of the six crystal systems.

Every crystalline mineral can be shown to be made of atoms which are arranged in one of these six repeating patterns, and so all crystals may be classified in this scheme. A mineral whose atoms are arranged in a cubic repeat pattern belongs to the cubic crystal system, and so on.

The six shapes of the building blocks are very special. They are the only shapes which can be used to build a solid three-dimensional object. Is it any wonder, then, that bricks, used in walls of houses, are the same shape as the orthorhombic building block of crystals? Any of the others could be used; but some of them, like the monoclinic and triclinic blocks, would result in a wall with sloping sides and would not be practical. These special shapes are the only ones which may be used to make regular three-dimensional solids (crystals). If any other shapes are used, the final result will have holes in it and so cannot be called solid.

How Crystals Are Built

Earlier in this chapter we mentioned that crystal faces correspond to the prominent planes in the atomic arrangement (usually called the crystal structure) of a mineral. In the galena structure model (Plate 1), there are three very prominent planes of atoms: those lying horizontally or flat, those standing vertically and seen end-on, and those standing vertically and seen side-on. These three planes are at right angles to one another and are parallel to the sides of a cube. Because they are the prominent planes of atoms, crystals of galena are commonly cube-shaped. Compare the shapes of

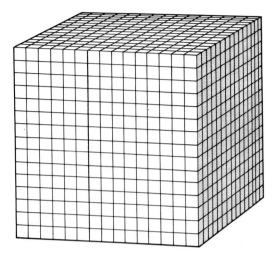

Fig. 2-8 Cube-shaped blocks make a cube-shaped crystal

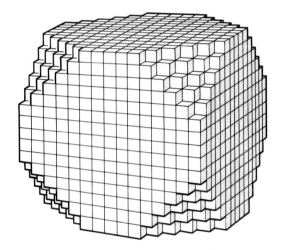

Fig. 2-9 Cube-shaped blocks incompletely stacked

Fig. 2-10 Cube-shaped blocks stacked to make an octahedron

the crystals in the galena specimen shown beside the model in Plate 1 and in Plate 2. In addition to the cube faces on galena crystals, other faces may occur parallel to other planes of atoms in the atomic arrangement (Plate 2).

We can relate the prominent planes of atoms in a crystal structure to the corners or sides of the building blocks. Fig. 2-8 shows the simplest and most obvious example—a cubic crystal built of cube-shaped blocks. Fig. 2-9 is very similar but the corners of the cubic crystal are left incomplete, although in a regular manner. Fig. 2-10 carries this to the extreme; the cube face is almost non-existent, and only the sloping faces are developed. This shape is called an *octahedron* and is another possible crystal shape in the cubic crystal system. Remember that the building blocks are very small indeed, therefore any crystal of a mineral contains many millions of these cubes and the individual blocks cannot be seen.

Symmetry

Any crystal, regardless of its shape or size, must be built from identically shaped building blocks corresponding to one of those shown in Fig. 2-7. Therefore that particular crystal must possess at least some of the characteristics of the building block which makes it. Each of the six building blocks looks different because each has different symmetry and the kind of symmetry is reflected in the shapes of the crystals which are developed from them. Symmetry of crystals is a difficult subject to discuss and will not be mentioned in detail here. However, it is important to know that by studying the symmetry of crystals it is possible to determine the type of building block which forms the crystal, and thus place it in one of the six crystal systems.

Most attempts to identify the true symmetry of a crystal can be done only by using complex instruments. A widely used instrument in the modern mineralogical laboratory is based on the use of X-rays. These X-ray techniques are very specialized and cannot be described here, but the method—called *X-ray diffraction*—when applied to crystals gives important information related to

33

the arrangements of their component atoms, and their symmetry.

Chemistry and Crystals

We know that crystals are made of atoms which are regularly arranged, and we can think of these arrangements in terms of the six different building-block shapes. This information concerns only the crystallography of the mineral being studied. Other important information relates to the kinds of atoms which make up the crystal. Thus we have two main aspects of crystals: the arrangements of the atoms and the kinds of atoms in the arrangement. Both aspects must be dealt with, in order that the mineral being studied may be described properly.

An outstanding example of this is the two minerals diamond (Fig. 2-11) and graphite. Both are composed of carbon atoms and so their chemical

Fig. 2-11 An octahedral diamond crystal (1 cm. on edge). It weighs 11-75 carats and comes from South Africa

properties are the same, but they have different *arrangements* of those atoms and so their physical properties are different. (This is dealt with in more detail later.) So, if we say only that a mineral is made of carbon atoms, there would be no way of telling whether we mean diamond or graphite; if, however, the arrangements of the atoms are mentioned, then the difference would be apparent. Another example are the minerals gold, silver and copper; all have the same arrangements of atoms in their crystal structures, but obviously they are not the same materials—they are each made of different kinds of atoms.

More About Crystals

There is something wonderful about crystals besides their beauty and colour. They have symmetry. Their faces are often smooth and mirror-like, and are arranged in a regular way. The symmetry of crystals is very difficult to describe without a great deal of explanation and so we can give here only the broad outlines.

Single Crystals

A single crystal contains atoms which are arranged in a regular and repetitive manner in three dimensions. Even if the crystal is very tiny, it contains millions of atoms, all regularly arranged. If there is no marked change in this arrangement, then the crystal is a single crystal. However, if a major change occurs in the arrangement from one part to another, then more than one crystal is present.

In the previous chapter we said that any one crystal is built from identically sized and shaped building blocks; we also said that any one crystal is built from only one of the six differently shaped blocks.

The way in which the atoms are arranged in a crystal is responsible for its outward shape; because the atoms are arranged regularly, the faces of the crystal also will be regular. By careful measurement of the angles between the faces of a crystal, it can be discovered that each crystal has symmetry which corresponds to the symmetry of one of the six simple building blocks. This is true no matter how complex the crystal appears to be. The principles of symmetry are therefore most important, and mineralogists and crystallographers study symmetry in order to describe crystals.

In 1669 the Dane, Nicolaus Steno, did the work which later was used to prove the *law of constant interfacial angles*. This law concerns the angles between the faces on crystals. His research involved the measurement of the angle between a particular pair of faces on quartz crystals. Using many different quartz crystals from many different places, he found that this angle was always the same. It was not until 1784 that the French mineralogist, the Abbé Haüy, offered an explanation. He concluded that a crystal was composed of identically shaped and sized, very tiny building blocks. Each mineral, he said, had its own unique building block, either in size and/or shape. The actual proof of his brilliant conclusion was not possible until the development of X-ray studies of crystals, which started about the beginning of this century.

The law of constant interfacial angles is an important one in mineralogy, since it concerns the symmetry of crystals and enables the student to place any crystal into one of the six crystal systems. Such symmetry studies are particularly useful in the identification of crystals of unknown minerals.

As mentioned in Chapter 2, X-ray techniques reveal the true symmetry of crystals. In addition to giving the symmetry, X-ray methods are used to work out the actual positions of the atoms in the crystal structure. Modern crystallographers are concerned more with these internal arrangements of atoms than with the external shapes of the crystals.

The study of single crystals externally by eye or microscope, and also internally by X-ray methods, usually gives the mineralogist enough information to identify them. Knowledge of the kinds of atoms in the structure of the crystal can be obtained by chemical analysis, and provides the final conclusive proof of its identity.

We shall now go on to describe crystals which are made up from more than one single crystal. These may involve just two crystals grown together, or many millions of tiny single crystals so small that they cannot be seen individually by the naked eye or even under the microscope.

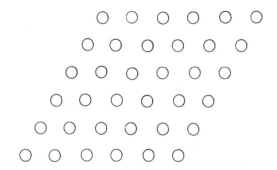

Fig. 3-1a   The arrangement of atoms in a single crystal

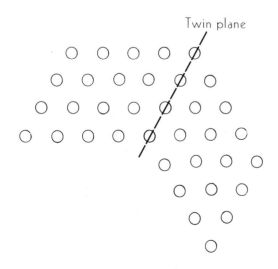

Fig. 3-1b   The same arrangement twinned

Twin plane

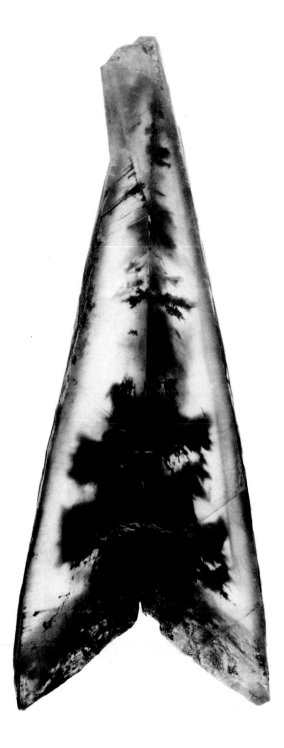

Twin Crystals

Twin crystals are composed of two or more single crystals. Those easiest to describe consist of only two crystals growing together in such a way that there is some regular relationship between the two. Fig. 3-1 shows a two-dimensional, regular arrangement of atoms in a single crystal (a), compared to the same arrangement in a twin crystal (b). You will notice that the pattern remains the same, but changes direction along a definite line. Of course in three dimensions the matter is not so simple, but usually the place where the direction of the pattern changes is defined by a plane rather than a line. This plane is called the twin plane.

Most twin crystals are given names which either describe their appearance or are named for the place where they were first discovered, for example, the Carlsbad twins of orthoclase. A gypsum swallow tail twin and a gypsum butterfly twin are shown in Figs. 3-2 and 3-3. In each of these you can see the distinct plane separating the two parts of the twin. Some twinned crystals appear as if the two parts are inter-grown with each other. These are called *interpene-tration* twins. Fluorite is a common example of this kind of twinning (Fig. 3-4). Another example is shown in the photograph of the dolomite twin (Plate 3).

Some twin crystals consist of more than two single crystals and so they have more than one twin plane. The mineral albite of the Plagioclase Group is an example; the twin planes in these minerals are parallel, and may be only fractions of an inch apart. Fig. 3-5 shows part of a twinned plagioclase specimen, the very fine straight lines representing the twin planes. Other twins which have more than one twin plane are the so-called *cyclic* twins. In these the twin planes are not parallel to each other, and the twin parts of the crystal appear to be arranged around a circle. A cyclic twin of cerussite is shown in Fig. 3-6.

There are other kinds of twins, many quite complex, but the essential fact of twinning is that the parts of the twin crystal bear a definite symmetry relation to each other.

Fig. 3-5   Fine twin planes in plagioclase,   ▷
fractions of an inch apart. Baffin Island, Canada

Fig. 3-4   Interpenetrating cubes of fluorite   ▽

Fig. 3-3   A gypsum "butterfly" twin, named for
its shape. Brazil

Fig. 3-6   Cyclic twins of cerussite. The straight
crystals are twinned at 120° to each other making
the "six-rayed" twin group. South West Africa

40

Fig. 3-7   Wavellite crystals usually appear as stellated aggregates. This specimen is from Barnstable, Devonshire, England, and is about 6 x 5 cm.

Crystal Aggregates

Few mineral specimens are single crystals or simple twin crystals. Most are aggregates of many crystals. Crystal aggregates are composed of many tens, hundreds, thousands or even millions of single crystals grown together. Unlike twin crystals, these do not bear any special symmetry relation from one crystal to the next. These aggregates are named to describe their appearance and, because some of these names are derived from Latin or Greek roots, they need some explanation. The more common ones are described and some are illustrated by photographs.

Your sugar bowl at home is a good place to develop a crystal aggregate. A drop of water will hold some of the crystals together and partly dissolve others. As the water evaporates, the dissolved sugar will crystallize again and cement the original grains into an aggregate. Of course, there is no special relationship between any of the crystals, but in natural crystal aggregates the crystals usually grew together at the same time, rather than by being cemented together later, although this also may happen.

Some crystal aggregates are identified easily as such, and each crystal can be seen clearly. Plate 4, of the mineral scolecite, shows a beautiful radiating group of long, slender needles, each one of which is a single crystal; together they make a radiating aggregate. Some minerals commonly occur as radiating aggregates and, if these are nearly complete and have a "starry" appearance, they are called *stellated* aggregates (Fig. 3-7). Now let us take another look at Plate 4 and imagine that there are many more crystals, and they are very much thinner and more tightly packed together. In fact, let us imagine that they are so small that they cannot be seen individually. The result would be a smooth rounded shape which is not a single crystal but is a crystal aggregate. The names used to describe this kind of aggregate depend on the size and shape.

Small, pea-sized, round aggregates, common in some specimens of calcite, are described as *pisolitic.*

Fig. 3-8   A specimen of botryoidal malachite from Reedy Creek, South Australia (8½ x 5 cm.)

42

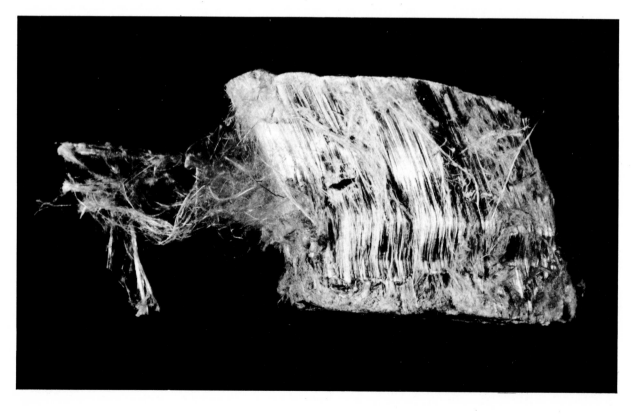

Smaller aggregates, consisting of round pellets, like heavy shot, are called *oolitic* aggregates. Some hematite shows this.

Mineral specimens which show a surface of rounded bumps about the size of grapes are called *botryoidal* aggregates (Fig. 3-8). Malachite shows this type of aggregate, and usually a detailed inspection will show that each bump consists of a radiating group of very fine needles. Plate 5 shows a polished section through some of these bumps in a specimen of malachite.

Reniform is another term for some types of rounded aggregates, where the shape of the aggregate is like a kidney. Hematite so commonly shows this shape that it is popularly called "kidney ore."

Tiny crystals may grow on top of one another to form an irregular line, from which branching lines of crystals may extend. The result is a tree-like shape and such aggregates are called *dendritic*. Native copper sometimes shows this (Fig. 3-9).

Minerals like chrysotile, a kind of asbestos, are made up of very fine hair-like crystals. Each fibre is a single crystal and they are all parallel to each other. These are called *fibrous* aggregates (Fig. 3-10).

Minerals which form *columnar* aggregates are made up of columns of crystals. Graphite is an example of a mineral which sometimes has this appearance.

Laminated minerals possess a definite platey structure which is recognized easily. They look like the leaves of a book. The Mica Group of minerals shows striking examples of this type of aggregate. Plate 6 displays this in the mineral muscovite. Poorly defined platey aggregates are described as *foliated*. Talc sometimes occurs as foliated aggregates.

A *granular* aggregate refers to groups of crystals which are shaped like rounded grains, much like the cemented sugar crystals described earlier. A mineral example is olivine.

Most mineral specimens are made up of aggregates of many single crystals. Few are single crystals alone. If the crystals in an aggregate are large, the specimen can be described as a crystal group. Many colour plates in this book show crystal groups.

If a mineral specimen is not clearly a crystal group, a twin crystal or a single crystal, it is probably a crystal aggregate. Some minerals escape detection as aggregates because the crystals in them are so small that they cannot be seen even with a good microscope. Agate is an example, and was at one time thought to be a distinct mineral species although it was known that it contained the same kinds of atoms as the mineral quartz. It was thought to be non-crystalline and to have a random arrangement of atoms. The final proof came through X-ray studies which showed conclusively that agate and quartz are indeed the same mineral. Therefore agate is considered only a variety of quartz and not a separate mineral species.

Pseudomorphs

This word refers to minerals which look like something that they are not. A good example is petrified wood (Fig. 3-10). It looks like wood but some examples are aggregates of millions of tiny quartz crystals. A piece of wood may become buried after the death of a tree and, later, circulating water in the ground, carrying silicon and oxygen atoms in solution, may surround it; the water will dissolve the woody material atom by atom and replace each little part with atoms of silicon and oxygen. In this way, after the process is complete, the finest detail of the wood is preserved; but the material is no longer wood, it is quartz (Plate 7).

Similar processes occur in many other different situations. Malachite, a copper mineral, rarely occurs in large crystals; but some, several inches long, have been found. A close examination of these and a study of their crystal shapes proved that the crystal was originally azurite (also a copper mineral) and not malachite. It seems likely that the malachite replaced the azurite bit by bit, thus preserving the original crystal shape but changing the chemistry. This example is said to be a *pseudomorph* of malachite after azurite.

Other examples of pseudomorphs are quite common. An interesting one is orthoclase, a mineral composed of potassium, aluminum and silicon atoms. Orthoclase occurs frequently as distinctive twinned crystals. These twins are

Fig. 3-12 Tiger eye (polished slab 12 x 5 cm.), a pseudomorph of quartz which has replaced asbestos. Notice the fine wavy "fibres" of the original asbestos which are now entirely quartz. Republic of South Africa

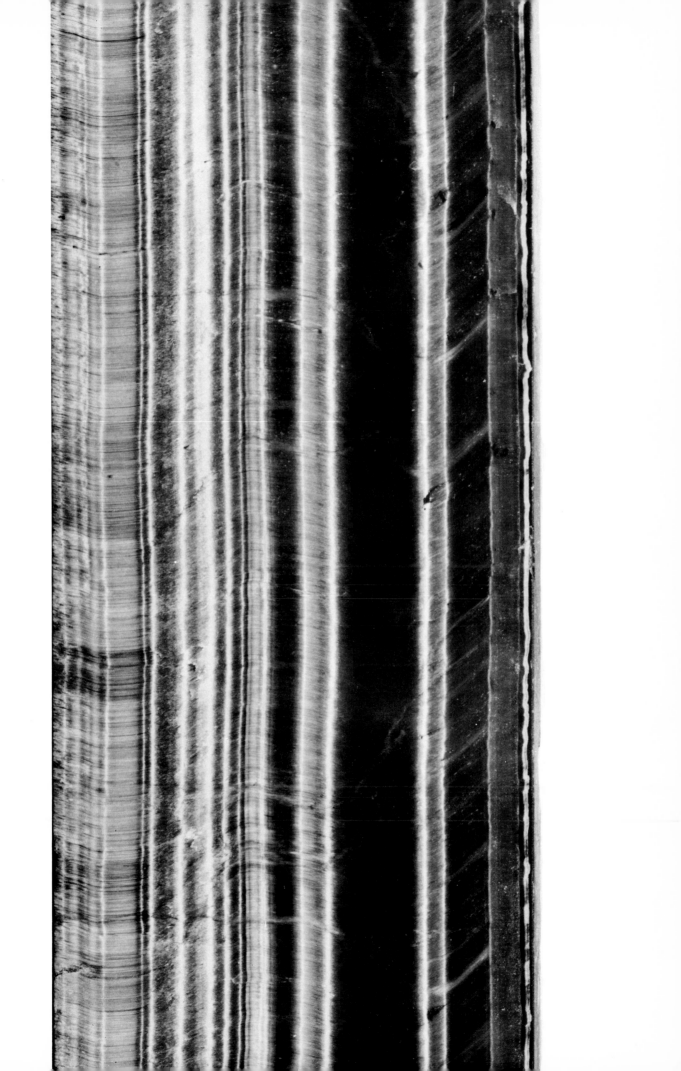

Fig. 3-11 This specimen of dolomite shows the unique crystal forms of twinned orthoclase. Therefore it is described as dolomite pseudomorphous after orthoclase. It comes from Kokomo, California, U.S.A., and is about 2 x 1½ cm.

characteristic of only this mineral and are called Carlsbad twins. Pseudomorphs of these twins are found occasionally and are made of minerals which are entirely different from orthoclase. Some of the known examples of orthoclase pseudomorphs are: cassiterite (a tin mineral) after orthoclase; topaz (an aluminum silicate containing fluorine) after orthoclase; dolomite (a calcium magnesium carbonate) after orthoclase (Fig. 3-11). None of these minerals has chemical compositions or crystal structures resembling orthoclase, yet they still occur as pseudomorphs after this mineral.

The semi-precious material, often called tiger eye, is a pseudomorph of a variety of asbestos which has been replaced by quartz. The minute scale of the replacement is shown by the fact that each individual fibre of the original asbestos-type mineral is preserved (Fig. 3-12).

Non-crystalline Minerals

GLASSES

Although most minerals are crystalline, there are a few which are not. One group of these minerals is called the *natural glasses*. An example is the mineral lechatelierite which is formed from quartz sand when it is struck by lightning. The sudden and tremendous amount of heat in a stroke of lightning is enough to melt the quartz sand and, since it is applied for only a short time, the molten quartz cools quickly and the silicon and oxygen atoms do not have time to arrange themselves into an orderly pattern. Thus the material consists of random arrangements of atoms and possesses a non-crystalline structure. With the passage of geologic time, however, the atoms may be able to re-arrange themselves and the glass eventually may crystallize.

THE METAMICT MINERALS

The *metamict* minerals, in general, are also non-crystalline. By definition, their atoms are arranged at random, and consequently no order exists in their crystal structures. They have the same character as the natural glasses but are formed in a completely different way.

However, some specimens of metamict minerals do show crystal faces. This can only be explained by

48

Fig. 3-13 A large, nearly perfect betafite crystal from the Silver Crater Mine, Hastings County, Ontario, Canada. The crystal measures $4\frac{1}{2} \times 4\frac{1}{2}$ cm.

the assumption that these minerals were crystalline when they were formed and that later events have destroyed their crystallinity. The metamict minerals contain various amounts of radioactive atoms in their structures, and it is thought that the high energy particles which are emitted by these radioactive atoms are powerful enough to break up the orderly arrangement of the crystal structure.

The use of X-rays in the study of metamict minerals is hampered by their non-crystallinity, since the X-ray method depends upon the material being crystalline. But some metamict minerals can be made to become crystalline by heating below the melting temperature. The heat enables the atoms in the mineral to move more easily and they sometimes re-arrange themselves into an orderly arrangement. However, it is not easy to prove that the crystal structure produced by heating the metamict mineral is the same as the crystal structure of the original mineral.

Some examples of metamict minerals are betafite (Fig. 3-13), priorite, fergusonite and aschynite. They can be recognized by a dark brown or black colour, and a glassy lustre; in fact they have the properties of glass in that they fracture with typically curved surfaces, and are brittle.

The Growth of Crystals

If we make a concentrated solution of copper sulphate in water, and then suspend a tiny copper sulphate crystal in the solution, the crystal will begin to grow. A dust-free container must be used for the experiment and a steady temperature ensured. After several weeks of growth, a large copper sulphate crystal will develop. The original "seed" crystal need be only a fraction of an inch long, but it may grow to more than two inches in length.

How Atoms Make Crystals

Crystals grow by placing the right kinds of atoms into the right kinds of arrangements. A crystal comprises a regular, three-dimensional array of many millions of atoms. Each of these atoms has to find its way into a particular position in the growing, three-dimensional pattern. Imagine a battalion of soldiers scattered about on a parade ground. At a command, each soldier begins to find his way to his proper place in the ranks, and soon all the soldiers form an orderly arrangement. We can think of the atoms in a solution as being scattered, with no regular arrangement. When crystallization begins, the atoms start to place themselves into definite positions and finally achieve a regular pattern. The soldiers on the parade ground form a two-dimensional pattern, but the atoms in a crystal build up a three-dimensional arrangement. As the soldiers form ranks only when told to, the atoms in a solution will form a regular arrangement only when they receive the order. Nature gives the order by providing suitable conditons for crystallization, such as the temperature and pressure of the solution. The right conditions will cause the atoms to find their correct places and thus form a crystal.

Fig. 4-1   Graphite, 11 x 5 cm. Quebec, Canada

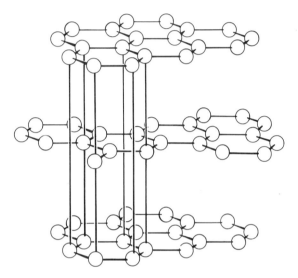

Fig. 4-2a   The arrangement of carbon atoms in graphite

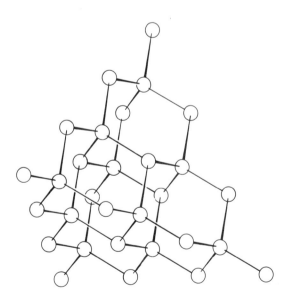

Fig. 4-2b   The arrangement of carbon atoms in diamond

Water is a common solution from which crystals may be formed. A solution of water (H_2O) and salt (NaCl), if left to evaporate, will produce tiny salt crystals when the water no longer can carry the salt dissolved in it. At first, the salt will be deposited on the container as small crystals. As further evaporation takes place, more and more salt crystallizes, some to form new crystals and some adding to the small crystals already formed. If we take special measures, we can grow a large single crystal.

An Example of Crystallization

We can study crystals in the laboratory and in their natural state. Both studies rely on the allied sciences of chemistry, physics and mathematics. The element carbon (chemical symbol: C), you remember, occurs as two minerals, diamond and graphite, each with different properties (Fig. 4-1). The carbon atoms in graphite are strongly bonded together to make layers, but these layers are weakly joined to each other (Fig. 4-2a). This arrangement produces its soft, flaky character. The easy slippage between the layers of atoms makes graphite useful as an additive to grease and oil for improved lubricating qualities.

Diamond also is composed of carbon atoms, but has quite different physical properties from those of graphite. In sharp contrast to graphite, the hardness and brilliance of the diamond are its greatest assets. The difference between them is due to the differing arrangements of carbon atoms in these two minerals. Diamond has its carbon atoms compactly arranged, each atom as close as possible to all the surrounding atoms (Fig. 4-2b). This compact arrangement of atoms in diamond gives the structure great physical stability and accounts for its hardness and abrasive power.

How did these two remarkably different forms of carbon come into being? The conditions that caused their growth are as different as the minerals themselves. Carbon can be made by heating wood and, if the temperature is high enough, the carbon atoms will arrange themselves into layers and form graphite crystals. Diamond also can be made in laboratories but requires a complex method worked

52

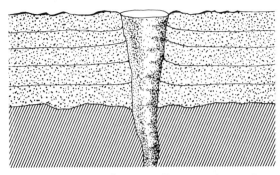

Fig. 4-3   A kimberlite pipe. These are large, the biggest known is about one mile in diameter

out from studies of natural diamond crystals and the rocks in which they formed.

In nature, diamond crystals occur in rocks called *kimberlite*, named for Kimberley, South Africa. These rocks are found in masses which are roughly circular at the surface and carrot-shaped in depth (Fig. 4-3). Geologists believe that these rocks came up to the earth's surface through volcanic pipes, and that the molten kimberlite rock originated at vast depths. The temperatures and pressures existing at these depths are great, and so we can conclude that the synthetic production of diamond requires similar conditions. If we compare the crystal structures of graphite and diamond (Figs. 4-2a and 2b), we can see that diamond has a more compact arrangement of carbon atoms than graphite; this implies that pressure also is important in changing graphite to diamond. Experiments using heat without pressure and experiments using pressure without heat were unsuccessful in producing diamond. But the use of both heat and pressure, properly applied to graphite, was successful.

Needless to say, the production of synthetic diamond and graphite is not as simple as described. The amount of heat and pressure required for the formation of diamond stretches the ingenuity of present-day technologists, and only small diamond crystals can be made economically. Other factors are involved in aiding the process of crystallization; time is important, and also the addition of other elements which, although not a part of the diamond structure, help the carbon atoms to arrange themselves into that structure.

Some of the aspects of crystal growth may be seen from the direct study of crystal specimens. We shall describe a few of these, which contain clues to the history of their formation.

A Phantom Quartz Crystal (Plate 8)

The quartz crystal in this photograph is called a *phantom crystal*. It shows internal growth stages which are marked by faint outlines of earlier crystals. The phantom outlines represent changes in the history of the development of the crystal, probably times when the crystal stopped growing and some other material was deposited as a dusting on the crystal faces; later the conditions changed again and the crystal was able to continue growing. The dust particles thus were trapped and marked a stage in the growth history of the crystal. If the dusting is light, the crystal may continue to grow; however, if the dusting is heavy and the crystal faces completely covered, it is unlikely that it will continue to grow as a single crystal. The quartz crystal in Plate 8 has many phantoms inside it, every one marking a stage in its history.

A Partial Phantom Calcite Crystal (Plate 9)

The calcite crystal shown in this illustration is a partial phantom crystal, since the last overgrowth stage is unfinished. The original crystal is the steep-sided "dog-tooth" variety which has been overgrown, in part, by a later growth of calcite. The faces of the earlier crystal, which are not covered by the overgrowth, are heavily dusted with a brown iron oxide. Careful examination of the other faces, which are overgrown, shows that the dusting is light. This suggests that the reason for the partial overgrowth is that the dusting on some of the faces covered the original calcite so completely that the incoming atoms of the late stage were unable to continue the growth of the first crystal. On the other faces, however, the dusting was light enough to leave some of the original calcite exposed and thus allow the newly arrived atoms to continue the growth of the original crystal; the atoms on the surface of the earlier crystal direct the new atoms into their proper positions. On the brown, heavily coated faces of the calcite, there is a thin layer of many hundreds of tiny calcite crystals which are not continuous with the original.

How did the original calcite crystal become unevenly coated? It is possible that the solution bringing the iron atoms of the dusting material was flowing from a particular direction and, as a result, the faces of the original calcite that were facing into the current received the heaviest coating, while those facing down-current received only a light dusting.

A Phantom Calcite Crystal (Plate 10)

The phantom in this calcite crystal is marked by inclusions of copper crystals. It is of special interest because the inner crystal is milky-white in colour while the outer calcite, deposited after the copper crystallized, is colourless. We could guess that after the original crystal began to grow, the solutions carrying the calcium (Ca) and carbonate (CO_3) atoms (of calcite) became weak and the crystal stopped growing. During this period, however, the solution also contained copper atoms, and the conditions were right for copper crystals to be deposited on the original calcite. This copper-rich solution was present, perhaps, for only a short time; or perhaps only a small amount of copper was present. Whatever the reason for the light dusting of copper, the conditions once more became suitable for the crystallization of calcite. Since the copper crystals formed only a light dusting on the faces of the milky-white crystal, the new crystal was able to continue the growth of the original, thus enclosing the copper crystals. The change in the conditions of growth is marked not only by the presence of the copper crystals, but also by the fact that the early calcite crystal is different from the later overgrowth. Some slight difference must have existed between the crystallizing conditions for each part of this crystal.

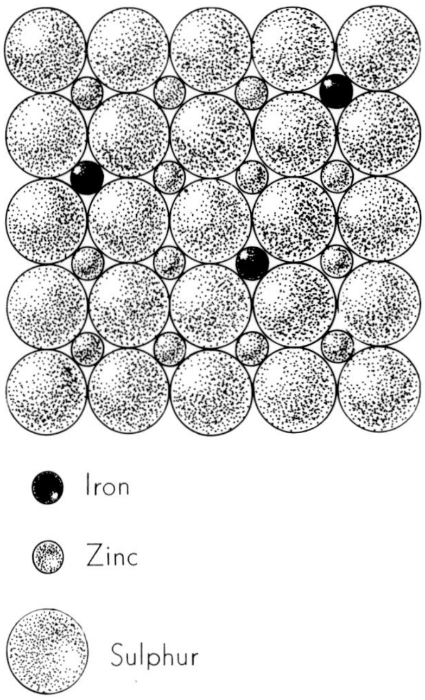

A Group of Barite Crystals (Plate 12)

The specimen shown in these photographs consists of bluish crystals of barite, placed at random on a mass of small, cream-coloured dolomite crystals. Also the specimen is lightly dusted with a coating of red hematite (an iron oxide). The two pictures show the same specimen viewed from different angles. The one picture shows a predominance of red, and the other scarcely any red at all. Like the partial calcite phantom crystal, this is an example of directional deposition. Perhaps a current in the crystallizing solution caused the hematite to form on only one side of the crystals of barite and dolomite, or the hematite may have crystallized from a standing solution and coated only the upward-facing sides of the existing barite crystals.

From the above discussions and illustrations we can see how much information can be obtained from just looking at mineral specimens. These are, however, particularly fine specimens and show their characteristic features very well. Such excellent

● Iron

◉ Zinc

◯ Sulphur

Fig. 4-4   A diagram showing how iron atoms can replace zinc atoms in crystal structures like sphalerite

55

specimens are rare, and most crystals have to be examined much more carefully before they give away any clues to their history.

Impure Crystals

Another interesting aspect of crystal growth is the presence of atoms foreign to the normal or ideal composition of the mineral. Pure sphalerite (ZnS), for instance, is composed of zinc and sulphur atoms in a definite arrangement. The size and chemical nature of iron (Fe) atoms is similar to zinc atoms and therefore they may replace some of the zinc atoms in the crystal structure of sphalerite. The chemical composition thus may be changed from ZnS to (Zn, Fe)S. This is illustrated by the diagram shown in Fig. 4-4.

Mineralogists and geologists have attempted to find out what conditions are required for sphalerite to take in certain amounts of iron atoms. One conjecture was that the amount of iron in the structure of natural sphalerite could be related to the temperature at which this mineral crystallized. If so, then this information could be used to help to discover other ore bodies. Unfortunately, the amount of iron in a sphalerite crystal is not related simply to the temperature of formation, and other factors are involved.

Other Inclusions in Crystals

In addition to phantom inclusions and chemical impurities, many natural crystals contain random inclusions of other minerals. These inclusions also can provide information about the physical and chemical conditions at the time of formation of the crystal. Some especially fascinating inclusions are made of gas and liquid. These are thought to have formed by irregularities of crystal growth which completely surrounded a part of the mineral-forming fluid, thus sealing it off and preserving it (Fig. 4-5). Some quartz crystals contain cavities filled with liquid, often with a gas bubble as well. Chemical analyses of these inclusions give valuable information about the chemistry of the solutions from which the quartz crystals grew. Although it is extremely difficult to extract the liquid and gas from a crystal cavity without contaminating them,

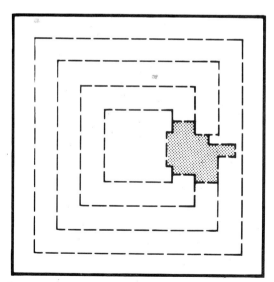

Fig. 4-5 A liquid inclusion, trapped by irregular growth stages inside a crystal

56

some successful studies have been made. Many other minerals contain liquid and gas inclusions, and special attention is being paid to those in ore minerals. Here again, the inclusions represent a sample of the ore-forming fluid which can provide clues to the chemistry of the ore-bearing solution. This information then can assist in discovering new ore deposits.

Crystal Shapes (Forms)

A certain mineral may occur in a wide variety of crystal shapes. At present we know little about why this should be so, and the problem requires much more study. Scientists have begun the study by using simple solutions of easily crystallized materials, such as copper sulphate and common salt. They have found that common salt will form crystals of one shape under some conditions and crystals of another shape under different conditions. Also, they have found that the addition of tiny amounts of certain elements and compounds to the crystallizing solutions may cause crystals of a certain shape to develop in preference to any other shape.

The mineral calcite is found in a wide variety of crystal forms. The partial phantom crystal (Plate 9) shows some of these. The inner crystal is the sharp-pointed "dog-tooth" variety, but the overgrowth has less steep faces at the top, which makes the end of the crystal blunt. This, too, suggests that the conditions of crystallization of the earlier crystal were slightly different from those of the later one.

Crystal Oddities

In addition to almost perfect crystals, there are a host of crystal oddities such as bent, curved and twisted crystals. Unless physical forces, such as bending, twisting or breaking, have occurred, most odd-shaped crystals can be explained as aggregates of crystals. Twisted quartz crystals can be explained in this way. They appear to be composed of many thin quartz crystals, each of which is turned slightly from one to the next; the amount of the "turn" from crystal to crystal is in the same direction, and roughly the same amount each time. The resulting aggregate appears to be a single

Fig. 4-6 A twisted quartz crystal, 5½ cm. high. Switzerland

Fig. 4-8 Skeletal quartz. Note the "hollow" faces at the top and the prominent edges between them. 24 cm. high. Brazil

Fig. 4-9 Small octahedral galena crystals in parallel growth on a cube of galena. Missouri, U.S.A.

Fig. 4-7 A sceptre quartz crystal, 44 cm. high. Actually this is a complex double crystal with a "coronet" of overgrown crystals, parallel to the centre crystals, showing parallel overgrowth

twisted crystal (Fig. 4-6). Other crystal oddities include *sceptre* crystals and *skeletal* crystals. Sceptre crystals are named for their shape—they are bigger at one end than at the other, and the larger crystal appears to be mounted on a thin stem (Fig. 4-7). Skeletal crystals have incomplete faces and their edges are pronounced, producing a skeletal appearance (Fig. 4-8).

Crystal Overgrowths

Although phantom crystals fall under this heading, other kinds of overgrowths exist. Fig. 4-9 shows a cube of galena which is overgrown with small octahedral crystals of the same mineral. The octahedral crystals are all lined up with one another, and their positions are controlled by the arrangement of atoms which make the cube.

In some instances the overgrowth mineral is different from the host mineral. Of special interest are those which are specially oriented in relation to each other. Such overgrowths represent a marked change in the nature of the crystallizing solutions: a change in chemistry, probably accompanied by changed conditions like temperature and pressure. An example, shown in Plate 11, is an overgrowth of chalcopyrite (composed of iron, copper and sulphur atoms) on sphalerite (composed of zinc and sulphur atoms). The photograph shows that all the brassy-coloured chalcopyrite crystals are arranged in an identical manner and are resting on a single, but imperfect, face of a sphalerite crystal (dark brown). The atomic arrangement of the zinc and sulphur atoms in the sphalerite crystal therefore influenced the positions in which the chalcopyrite crystals grew.

The Physical Properties of Minerals —1

The physical properties of minerals can be determined without the use of chemical tests. They depend upon the kinds and arrangements of atoms in their crystal structures. Transparency, lustre, colour, specific gravity, hardness, cleavage, fracture, magnetic properties, electrical properties, radioactive and optical properties are all physical. We can use most of these properties for quick identifications of minerals, although this should be confirmed with additional chemical and crystallographic information.

Transparency

Transparency is the term used to describe the ease with which we can see through a mineral. Three terms are in common use: *opaque* minerals are those through which no light can be seen; *transparent* minerals are those which can be seen through clearly; *translucent* minerals are those through which a little light can be seen, intermediate between the terms opaque and transparent.

For most purposes this property is descriptive and is rarely measured. In describing a mineral, which might appear to be opaque, we must take care to examine the thin edges to see if, in thin fragments, it is translucent or transparent. Since minerals are rarely pure, different samples of the same mineral may show different degrees of transparency. A description of a certain mineral, therefore, may read translucent to transparent. Some transparent minerals are: quartz, calcite, beryl, diamond and gypsum, though it is essential to have pure, clean crystals to show this. Most of these examples of transparent minerals may be translucent also, especially if they are impure, or are not perfect crystals. Lightly coloured minerals, as well as colourless minerals, may be transparent. Some examples of opaque minerals are: silver, copper, galena and pyrite.

The kinds and arrangements of atoms in the crystal structure of the mineral determine whether or not light can be transmitted through them. In the transparent minerals, light waves striking the specimen make the atoms vibrate. This vibration is passed from atom to atom through the structure and, at the other side, the vibrations produce similar light waves. Opaque minerals have atomic arrangements which are unable to transmit the light waves, and the vibration of the atoms is absorbed quickly by their arrangement; thus the light is absorbed, and not transmitted through the mineral. Translucent minerals allow some of the light to be transmitted, but some is absorbed.

Many transparent minerals of suitable colours and hardnesses are cut and polished into attractive gemstones. Diamond and topaz are examples. Quartz is used for the production of lenses for special optical instruments. Of course, only well-formed transparent crystals can be used.

Lustre

The lustre of a mineral refers to its surface appearance. Like transparency, it is not usually measured.

There are two major categories. Those minerals which look like metals have a metallic lustre. All other minerals have a non-metallic lustre. There are no other descriptive words for the metallic minerals. The non-metallic minerals, however, are referred to by various terms which describe their surface appearance. Some are mentioned here with mineral examples: *pearly* (gypsum), *vitreous* or glassy (quartz), *greasy* (nepheline), *silky* (chrysotile asbestos), *waxy* (serpentine), *resinous* (sphalerite). Other terms are: *adamantine*, referring to a brilliant lustre like that of diamond; *earthy*, used for minerals like kaolin and the clay minerals, which appear dull.

Like transparency, lustre depends upon the ways in which the atoms and their arrangements affect the incoming light waves. Although some of the illuminating wavelengths of light may be either transmitted or absorbed, some light is reflected from the surface of the mineral. These reflected waves are responsible for the surface appearance of the mineral. The kinds and arrangements of atoms affect the character of the reflected light, and thus cause different lustres. Both diamond and graphite are composed of carbon atoms, but graphite is metallic and diamond is adamantine. The difference in lustres is due to the arrangements of atoms in these two mineral structures.

Colour

In general, few minerals have characteristic colours by which they can be recognized. Many show a wide variety of colours and shades of colours. Ordinary light (white light) is composed of many different wavelengths. Each wavelength corresponds to a colour of the spectrum. Combinations of wavelengths give rise to other, intermediate colours.

Although usually descriptive, colour can be measured by determining the wavelengths of light which are transmitted by the specimen, and the instrument used to do this is called a *spectrometer*.

Metallic minerals generally are of constant colour unless some surface alteration or tarnish has occurred. Thus specimens of molybdenite from all over the world are a bluish-steely-grey. Bornite, however, is rarely untarnished and it is necessary to chip off a small fragment to reveal the true colour. The colour of the tarnish, however, may be characteristic; and some metallic minerals may be recognized by the colour of their tarnish. Non-metallic minerals usually vary in colour. Fluorite, for instance, can be blue, purple, green, pink, brown, orange, yellow, colourless, and almost black. Quartz (Plate 13), calcite and many other minerals, also have a wide range of colours. A few non-metallic minerals do show nearly constant colour; some examples are sulphur (yellow), malachite (green) and azurite (blue).

We have seen that the colour of minerals depends upon the wavelengths of light which are transmitted through them or reflected from their surfaces. Some minerals have colours that are due to combi-nations of both effects. Transparent minerals, which transmit some light waves, may absorb others. This causes a change in the transmitted wavelengths and produces a certain colour. The amount and kind of change of wavelength which occurs depends upon the kinds and arrangements of atoms in the crystal structure. Clear, colourless quartz (composed of silicon and oxygen atoms) transmits all wavelengths of light illuminating it. Thus, if white light strikes the specimen, white light is transmitted. The purple colour of amethyst (a variety of quartz) is thought to be due to minute amounts of titanium and manganese atoms in the framework of the silicon and oxygen atoms. The presence of the titanium and manganese atoms causes slight defects in the crystal structure and causes some of the wavelengths to be absorbed, so that only those which represent purple are transmitted. The iron atoms in sphalerite (see Chapter 4, page 56) also cause structural defects which change the colour of the specimen, depending upon the amounts of iron atoms present. Pure sphalerite is usually yellow but, with increasing amounts of iron, the colour changes to brown; and with maximum iron content, the mineral is black.

It has been shown that colour in minerals can be due to the presence of elements foreign to the normal make-up of the mineral. However, experiments also have shown that we can change the colour by purely physical means, for example, by bombarding the mineral with X-rays or heating it. Amethyst turns brown when heated. This treatment results in no chemical change. The explanation of this must lie in defects produced by the heat or the X-rays in the crystal structure of the mineral. These defects upset the vibrations of the atoms and prevent the trans-mission of the usual wavelengths through the specimen, thus changing its colour.

Certain minerals have colour simply because they contain inclusions of another mineral. Colourless calcite, containing tiny needles of green hornblende, will be green. If the "foreign" crystals are large enough, close examination will show that the colour is due to them; but some minerals contain extremely minute inclusions, so evenly distributed that it is difficult to see that they are the cause of the colour.

Less variable than the colour of the actual specimen is the colour of the powdered mineral. We can use a simple technique to get a small sample of powder; the specimen is rubbed across a plate of white unglazed porcelain, and the smear is a sample of the powdered mineral. The colour of this powder can be described and is called the *streak* of the mineral. Quartz may be seen in a variety of colours —deep purple, yellow, black or smoky, colourless, rose, white (milky)—but the colour of the streaks of all these is white. The streaks of some minerals, however, do vary. Sphalerite (ZnS), when pure, gives a pale yellow streak. With increasing amounts of iron replacing zinc atoms in the structure, the streak, as well as the colour, darkens to brown. At the maximum iron content, when the specimens are black, they have a dark brown streak.

Another reason for the variation in colour of the streak is the presence of tiny crystals of another mineral included in the host mineral. The streak of such a mixture will reflect the colour combination of the streaks of the two minerals.

In general, colour is one of the most popular guides to the identity of minerals but, unfortunately, it is not reliable. The colour of the streak of the mineral lessens the variations and provides a more constant colour for more accurate identifications.

From prehistoric times, coloured minerals have been used for the colouring of paints. Nowadays, however, we usually use synthetic compounds. Small fragments of coloured minerals may be used to make mosaic designs and pictures. Coloured minerals used as gemstones are especially fascinating.

Fluorescence

Normally, the word *fluorescence* is reserved to describe the property of some minerals which glow in the dark when exposed to long or short wave ultraviolet light. Ultraviolet light (abbreviated to UV light) is a form of radiation like ordinary light, and consists of various wavelengths. The wavelengths of both long and short wave UV light are, however, very much shorter than normal light. Pure UV light is invisible; but most sources of UV light are imperfect, and give out some visible blue light. Non-fluorescent materials, therefore, may appear to have a slight bluish tint under a UV light. Fluorescent minerals exhibit a wide range of brilliant, and usually exotic, colours when exposed to UV light. The various colours produced may be used to identify certain minerals.

The property of fluorescence is usually descriptive; we can measure it only with the aid of costly instruments. A proper description usually includes the appearance of the mineral in long wave as well as short wave UV light. Lamps are available commercially which can produce both kinds of UV light and are essential for determining this property.

The fluorescent colours of minerals are produced in the same way as the colours of minerals when they are viewed in ordinary light. The colours are due to a change in wavelength. Fluorescent minerals which are exposed to invisible UV light have crystal structures which can change the wavelengths of the incoming, invisible UV light, reflecting them back as longer wavelengths, which are visible. This is why fluorescent minerals appear to glow in the dark. The visible light that is produced by the mineral often consists of unusual combinations of wavelengths which normally are not seen. This accounts for their exotic and "unreal" colours.

The power of some minerals to cause fluorescence is, in some instances, a property that is common to all specimens of a certain mineral. An example is the mineral scheelite. Others exhibit the property only in some specimens. Fluorite almost always fluoresces but calcite is usually non-fluorescent; however, some specimens of calcite fluoresce a deep pink or red in UV light. Since normal calcite does not fluoresce, the specimens which do must be unusual. The explanation lies in defects in the crystal structure due to the presence of "foreign" atoms in the structure. Atoms of manganese are usually responsible. The presence of these atoms causes slight distortions in the arrangement, and these are enough to change the kinds of wavelengths which are reflected off the specimen. Some minerals fluoresce one colour in long wave UV light, and another colour in short wave UV light. Thus different wavelengths striking the specimen are affected differently by its crystal structure.

Fluorescent minerals are in great demand by collectors because of the beauty of their extraordinary colours. Many uranium minerals, usually colourful in ordinary light, are even more brilliant when viewed under UV light. In some mining operations for fluorescent minerals, the concentration process involves passing the broken ore from the mine under a UV light. In this way the valuable minerals can be selected from the waste. The brilliant colours used in some dyes are fluorescent in character, the small amount of UV light in sunlight being enough to add a glowing brightness to them.

Phosphorescence

Phosphorescence may be defined as the property of a few minerals to continue to glow after the source of UV radiation has been removed. Although the colour of the phosphorescence can be described, its mere presence in a mineral is a clue to its identity. The luminous dials of some clocks and watches are made of phosphorescing materials, but the phosphorescence in this instance is excited by normal white light.

When UV light strikes the mineral, the atoms begin to vibrate, giving out visible light. If the atoms are in a considerable state of vibration, they may continue to vibrate and emit visible light after the UV light is removed. Phosphorescence is usually short-lived, lasting only a few minutes.

Specific Gravity

Some minerals are heavier than others. Their relative weights are a measure of their *specific gravity*. Since specific gravity (abbreviation SG) is relative, the weight of the mineral must be compared with a standard material. So we take water as this standard and give it an SG = 1.00. Materials which have an SG less than 1.00 will float on water; those with a greater SG will sink. Hence the specific gravity of a mineral may be defined as the weight of the specimen compared to the weight of an equal volume of water. For example, copper is about nine times heavier than water and has an SG = 8.90. The SG of gold is about 19.0, more than twice as heavy as an equal volume of copper, and nineteen times heavier than an equal volume of water.

Few minerals have precisely the same SG, so we can use this property as a means of identification if we make accurate measurements. The following steps and precautions illustrate a method of measuring SG:

1. A pure, clean specimen of the mineral must be selected.
2. That specimen must be weighed accurately on a chemical balance.
3. The specimen must then be suspended from a thread (or fine wire) attached to the beam of the balance, and immersed in a container of water.
4. The weight shown by the balance for the specimen in water is recorded. (Care must be taken to ensure that the specimen is not touching the sides of the container, and that there are no bubbles adhering to it.)
5. The weight of the specimen immersed in water will be less than its weight in air. The difference between these two measurements will be equal to the weight of a volume of water, which is equal to the volume of the specimen.
6. The following formula is used to calculate the specific gravity:

$$SG = \frac{\text{Weight of specimen in air}}{\text{Weight of an equal volume of water}}$$

Given the above precautions, the resulting value for the SG of the mineral will be quite accurate. With less accurate weighing instruments, we can obtain a reasonable approximation to the SG of the mineral in the same way. A rough guess of the SG can be made, after some experience is gained, by "hefting" specimens of various minerals by hand. This, of course, is very inaccurate; but it is enough to say whether the mineral is light, medium or heavy.

To explain the reasons for the differences in weight between various minerals, we must examine their crystal structures, and also the kinds of atoms present. Since some atoms are heavier than others, heavy minerals are, in general, those which contain heavy atoms. Two minerals which illustrate this are fluorite (SG = 3.1) and uraninite (SG = 10.0).

Both these minerals have the *same arrangements* of atoms, but contain *different kinds* of atoms (Plate 14). Fluorite is composed of calcium and fluorine atoms (CaF_2), and uraninite contains uranium and oxygen atoms (UO_2). The calcium and uranium atoms are nearly the same size, as are the fluorine and oxygen atoms. The following table compares the sizes and weights of these atoms in the two minerals.

Atom	Size (Å)	Atomic Weight	Number of atoms in the Formula	
Uranium (U)	0.97	238	1	Uraninite
Oxygen (O)	1.32	16	2	
Calcium (Ca)	1.18	40	1	Fluorite
Fluorine (F)	1.33	19	2	

Total atomic weight of $UO_2 = 238 + (2 \times 16) = 270$
Total atomic weight of $CaF_2 = 40 + (2 \times 19) = 78$
The total weight of the atoms in uraninite is a little more than three times that of the weight of the atoms in fluorite.

The fluorine atom is only slightly heavier than the oxygen atom, but the uranium atom is much heavier than the calcium atom. Thus we can say that uraninite has a greater SG than fluorite because of the presence of the heavy uranium atom. Note that the total atomic weights of these two minerals are such that the uraninite (SG = 10.0) is about three times heavier than fluorite (SG = 3.1). The slight difference in the calculated values and the actual values are due mainly to the slight differences in size between the calcium and uranium atoms, and the fluorine and oxygen atoms.

The two minerals graphite and diamond illustrate another reason for differences in SG between one mineral and another. Both are composed entirely of carbon atoms, but diamond is about one and a half times as heavy as graphite. This must be due to the arrangements of the atoms. We know that in graphite the carbon atoms are in layers which are comparatively far apart from each other (Fig. 4-2a), and that in diamond the carbon atoms are placed more compactly with a minimum of space between them (Fig. 4-2b). Because of this there are more carbon atoms in a certain volume of diamond than there are in the same volume of graphite. This provides another example of the effect of the atomic arrangements on the physical properties of minerals.

To sum up, there are two ways of using the atomic arrangements of minerals to explain the differences in specific gravity. One is the simple fact that some atoms are heavier than others; and the other is that either more or less atoms are packed into a certain volume, and this makes for a higher or a lower specific gravity. In most instances a combination of both these factors is involved.

The difference in weight between minerals is a physical property which has been put to practical use. Gold grains can be separated from quartz sand by the simple technique of washing in water. Running water is passed over the mixture, and the lighter quartz grains are picked up more easily than the gold and are washed away. Thus, by controlling the speed of the current of water, the quartz can be removed, leaving the gold. This technique is used by prospectors to pan gravels for heavy minerals. On a much larger scale, the same principle is used in some mine concentrating plants for the extraction of heavy minerals. Another technique, frequently employed in the laboratory, is the use of heavy liquids for separating one mineral from another. Certain liquids are available which have a high SG; thus by using a liquid of SG about 3.0, diamond (SG = 3.52) will sink, while the bulk of the remaining minerals (quartz sand, for example, with SG = about 2.65) will float.

The Physical Properties of Minerals — 2

This chapter continues the descriptions of the physical properties of minerals started in Chapter 5. Under each heading there is a definition, a means of describing or measuring the property, and an explanation of it and its uses.

Hardness

We can define hardness as the ability of a mineral to resist scratching; this is different from the ease with which it can be broken. Diamond is one of the hardest materials known but it can be shattered easily. The hardness of minerals can be measured and is a useful clue to their identification. Like the other physical properties, it is dependent upon the kinds and arrangements of atoms in mineral structures.

To measure the hardness of minerals, a set of standard materials of known hardness is used (Fig. 6-1). These standards may be common objects or a set of minerals of varying hardnesses. A hardness scale was devised by Mohs which ranges from 1 to 10, each value being represented by a mineral.

The inclusion of some common objects, with their approximate hardnesses, in the list of hardness materials is helpful, since these items are as useful as the hardness minerals in measuring the hardness of an unknown mineral. The first nine minerals in the scale are all common, and can be bought in small sets. Each specimen is a clean, pure fragment of the mineral and can be used to determine the hardness of an unknown mineral. For example, if the unknown is scratched by fluorite (H = 4) but not by calcite (H = 3), then the hardness of the unknown is about $3\frac{1}{2}$.

Fig. 6-1   This is a set of hardness points each set with a tiny chip of the five hardest minerals in the Mohs Scale. From left to right they are: orthoclase (H = 6), quartz (H = 7), topaz (H = 8), corundum (H = 9) and diamond (H = 10)

Mohs Hardness Scale is given below:

Mineral	Relative Hardness (H)
Talc	1
Gypsum	2
(fingernail, 2¼)	
Calcite	3
(copper coin, 3)	
Fluorite	4
Apatite	5
(steel knife blade, 5½)	
Orthoclase	6
(steel file, 6)	
Quartz	7
Topaz	8
Corundum	9
Diamond	10

When we perform a hardness test we must take certain precautions. The surface of the unknown mineral, which is to receive the scratch, must be clean and smooth. The test mineral used to do the scratching must have a clean, sharp edge. A check must be made after every test to see if, in fact, it did make a scratch because some soft minerals will leave a streak on the harder mineral which may only look like one. Any powder produced by the test must be wiped off and the scratch actually seen through a hand lens, before a conclusion can be reached. If there is a scratch, the test mineral is harder than the unknown. In general, a systematic approach is advisable, beginning with the softest test minerals and working toward the harder ones. In this way, a minimum of scratching will appear on the surface of the unknown and, if it is a fine crystal, little damage will be done. The test scratch need not be more than a fraction of an inch long, not scored right across the unknown specimen. After the hardness has been determined, it can be confirmed by using a clean, sharp edge of the unknown mineral to try to scratch test minerals of greater and lesser hardnesses.

Mohs Hardness Scale is relative, which means that calcite is not exactly three times as hard as talc, nor is diamond ten times as hard as talc. The scale merely lists ten minerals, each of which is harder than the one before it. The true hardness of these minerals is quite surprising, and is shown in Fig.

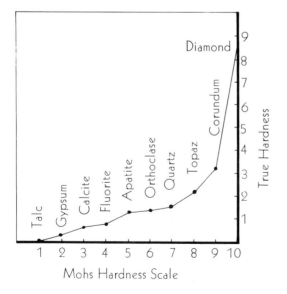

Fig. 6-2   True hardness compared with Mohs Hardness Scale

6-2. Note that diamond is about four times as hard as corundum. The true or absolute hardness of minerals can be measured with delicate instruments.

The hardness of minerals depends upon the kinds of atoms in them, and the ways in which they are arranged. Both diamond and graphite are composed of the same kinds of atoms, but they differ greatly in hardness. Diamond is the hardest of all natural materials, while graphite is among the softest. The explanation rests in the arrangements of the carbon atoms in these two minerals. We know that the carbon atoms of graphite are in layers, each layer weakly bonded to the next (Fig. 4-2a), and that, in contrast, the diamond structure has carbon atoms which are as closely packed as possible and strongly bonded to each other (Fig. 4-2b). The differences in these arrangements account for the differences in hardness between these two minerals. In general, the closer together the atoms are in a structure, the more resistance it will offer to scratching, and if the atoms are more widely spaced, the mineral is likely to be soft. To some extent also, the smaller the atoms are in a structure, the harder the material.

In most crystals, the arrangements of the atoms are slightly different in different directions. Because of this, a mineral may be harder in one direction than in another. Kyanite is the mineral usually used to illustrate this feature (Plate 15). Crystals of kyanite usually occur as long flat blades; they are softer parallel to the blades, about $4\frac{1}{2}$, than they are across the blades where they are about $6\frac{1}{2}$. Diamond also exhibits this difference in hardness with direction. The octahedral faces are the hardest, since in these planes the atoms are the most densely packed. The cube planes in diamond are the softest, since these directions represent the least compact arrangement of atoms. However, this does not affect the fact that both these directions in diamond are harder than any other known mineral.

The hardness of minerals has practical uses. Diamond is used as an abrasive and cutting material. Garnet sand is used to make sandpaper, and carborundum (a synthetic material) is used as an abrasive grit for grinding and polishing. Diamond-cutters use diamond powder to cut and polish diamonds. Soft minerals like talc often are used, in a finely ground form, as a base for face powders and cosmetics because of their non-abrasive qualities.

Tenacity

Tenacity refers to the breaking strength of minerals, not to the hardness. Gold is a soft mineral, but it requires great force to break it.

Various terms are used in mineralogy to describe the tenacity of minerals. Malleable minerals are those which can be beaten into thin sheets without breaking; copper (Fig. 6-3) and gold are examples. In contrast, brittle minerals shatter to pieces when struck sharply; diamond and quartz are examples. Some soft minerals, such as argentite (a silver mineral), can be cut with a knife into thin shavings. Argentite is described as being *sectile*. Elastic minerals, like muscovite, can be bent but will spring back to their original shape when the bending force is removed. Flexible minerals can be bent, but remain distorted after the force is removed; thin plates of gypsum illustrate this property.

Any force applied to a mineral will tend to strain the bonds between the atoms. In metals like gold and copper, the bonds between the atoms can adjust easily to new positions, and thus the mineral will break only with difficulty. On the other hand, when quartz is stressed, the bonds between the atoms resist breakage to a point, and beyond that they break suddenly, causing the mineral to shatter.

Tenacity can have various practical applications. Small pieces of gold can be hammered into extremely thin sheets to make gold leaf, which is used for decoration and sign-writing. The amount of gold used is so small that the cost is low.

Cleavage

Cleavage refers to the property of some minerals to break evenly along one or more special directions, leaving a smooth, flat surface. Minerals of the Mica Group are excellent examples showing a perfect cleavage; they can be split easily into very thin sheets.

We usually describe cleavage directions in a mineral in terms of their positions relative to its crystal faces. In some minerals which possess more

Fig. 6-3   Part of this specimen of natural copper has been hammered to illustrate the property of malleability. It comes from Michigan, U.S.A., and is 9 x 9 cm.

than one cleavage direction, the angles between these directions can be measured, as well as their relation to the crystal faces.

Cleavage results when a plane of weakness exists between the planes of atoms in a crystal structure. Since all crystal structures are regulated by the rules of repetition of atoms in three dimensions, the cleavage directions also must be regular and be closely related to those arrangements. However, mineral specimens with many parallel cleavages possess only one cleavage direction. Note that the *number of different directions of cleavage* is important, not the number of cleavages. Some minerals which possess only one good cleavage direction are: graphite, the Mica Group of minerals, talc, orpiment and topaz. Their crystal structures all possess a prominent plane of weakness in one crystallographic direction. In graphite, this plane of weakness is between the layers of carbon atoms (Fig. 4-2a); in the mica-type minerals, it is parallel to the strong planes of silicon and oxygen atoms, these planes being weakly joined to each other (Fig. 8-9).

Some minerals which have two directions of cleavage are those belonging to the Pyroxene Group (example: augite) and those belonging to the Amphibole Group (example: hornblende). Both these groups of minerals have similar chemistry and appearance, but they can be distinguished from each other by their cleavage directions (Fig. 6-4). Augite is composed of various elements holding together complex chains of silicon and oxygen atoms. These strong chains run parallel to each other through the mineral, and the cleavages occur between them. The arrangement of the chains is such that the angle between the two cleavage directions, in augite, is nearly 90 degrees. In hornblende the chains are double the width of those in augite; they also run parallel to each other in the structure, and the cleavage directions also run between them. Because of the greater width of these chains, the angle between the cleavage directions is nearly 120 degrees. These differences are shown in the diagram in Fig. 6-4.

Some minerals show three prominent cleavage directions. Galena and halite (common salt) are examples. Both these minerals have the same

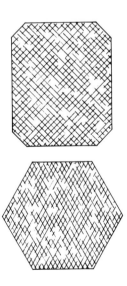

Fig. 6-4   Cleavage directions in augite at about 90° (top) and hornblende about 120° (bottom)

73

Fig. 6-5 Fragments of galena. Note the right-angled breaks representing the perfect cubic cleavage of this mineral

atomic arrangements, though they contain different kinds of atoms. Because of this, they have the same cleavages. The atoms occur in prominent planes which are at right angles to each other. The cleavage directions are between these planes. When a piece of galena is broken, most of the fragments will have right-angled sides, like little cubes (Fig. 6-5).

Calcite also has three cleavage directions, but they are not at right angles to one another. They are parallel to the faces of a rhombohedron, which looks like a "squashed" cube (Fig. 6-6).

Minerals with four cleavage directions (fluorite) and six cleavage directions (sphalerite) also can be explained in terms of planes of weakness in their atomic arrangements along certain directions.

A practical use of cleavage in minerals is well illustrated by diamond. That mineral possesses perfect cleavage parallel to the faces of an octahedron. Thus the diamond-cutter can select a flawless, perfect part from a natural crystal by cleaving it. In this way he can avoid costly cutting operations and wastage. Before cleaving a diamond, the cutter studies the crystal closely to determine the exact cleavage directions. A bladed instrument, called a cleaver, is placed along the precise direction of the cleavage and tapped sharply. If the position of the cleaver is correct, the diamond will break easily leaving a smooth, flat surface. If an error has been made, the diamond may shatter into many pieces because, although it is hard, it is also brittle.

Fracture

In the previous section we saw that cleavage occurs between planes of weakly bonded atoms in the mineral's crystal structure. Because of this, cleavage is closely related to the crystallography of the mineral. Fracture describes the appearance of the surfaces of minerals which have been broken *across* the planes of atoms. In contrast to cleavage, fracture is not related to special directions within a crystal structure.

Fracture describes the appearance of the broken surface and cannot be measured. We use various descriptive terms. A *conchoidal fracture* (Fig. 6-7) can

74

be recognized by concentric sets of cracks, which are dish-shaped and either concave or convex. This type of fracture is often seen in broken pieces of thick glass. Quartz, too, possesses this kind of fracture. The metallic elements, such as gold, silver and copper, when broken reveal a characteristic surface which is called a *hackly fracture*. Other terms, such as a *splintery fracture* are self-explanatory.

Minerals which do not possess cleavage have no prominent planes of weakness between the planes of atoms. Quartz, for example, is composed of a tightly bonded framework of silicon and oxygen atoms; any breakage which occurs results in the appearance of curved fractures. This is because no particular direction will break more easily than another. The hackly fracture of some of the native metals arises from the fact that the bonds between the atoms are able to adjust to new positions when under strain; the result is that, when the metal is broken, the pieces pull apart rather than break, leaving the curiously shaped hackly fracture.

Minerals possessing conchoidal fracture were used by prehistoric man; a sharp impact on a piece of flint, for example, could produce sharp-edged shards, useful for cutting or as scraping implements. Also by careful chipping of a flint pebble, they could fashion arrowheads or spear points.

Fig. 6-6   All the faces on this specimen are cleavages. They are not at right angles

Magnetic Properties

Magnetic properties refer to the ways in which minerals react when placed in a magnetic field; some are strongly attracted to the magnet, others less so, and some are slightly repelled.

Those minerals which are strongly attracted by a magnet are said to be *ferromagnetic* (examples are pyrrhotite and magnetite). Those which are weakly attracted are *paramagnetic* (examples are hematite, biotite, beryl and hornblende), and those which are slightly repelled are called *diamagnetic* minerals (examples are fluorite, calcite and quartz). In general, we cannot determine these differences without the use of a powerful electromagnet; however, we can use a small hand magnet to see if the mineral is attracted to it or not. Those which are attracted are ferromagnetic; those which are not are either paramagnetic or diamagnetic; we cannot

distinguish between the latter two, and usually call them non-magnetic.

A mineral which is attracted to a magnet must contain ferromagnetic or paramagnetic elements. Iron and nickel are examples of ferromagnetic elements, and their presence is usually responsible for the magnetism of some minerals. However, the actual orientations of the atoms in the structure are just as important as their presence. Two minerals, magnetite and hematite, both composed of iron and oxygen atoms, have very different magnetic qualities. Magnetite is strongly ferro-magnetic and small pieces will jump to the hand magnet. Hematite appears to be non-magnetic.

The explanation of the reactions of magnetite and hematite lies in the orientations of the iron atoms. Iron atoms have magnetic poles which may be compared to the magnetic poles of an ordinary magnet. If the atoms are arranged so that all the "north poles" lie in the same direction, they will reinforce one another and the mineral will be ferromagnetic and react like magnetite. If, however, the "north poles" are arranged at random throughout the structure, their magnetic effect will be cancelled and the mineral will be paramagnetic (hematite). Simplified diagrams to illustrate this are shown in Fig. 6-8.

The magnetic properties of minerals have some important practical applications. One of these is the separation of minerals from each other in the laboratory. In this way pure samples can be obtained for study purposes. An instrument is required, called a magnetic separator, which is a powerful electromagnet. The electric current applied to the magnet can be varied, and so different degrees of magnetism can be used. Thus minerals which are more attracted to the magnet can be removed from those which are less attracted. By careful adjustments of the instrument settings, most minerals can be separated even from complex mixtures of many minerals.

Electrical Properties

Electrical properties refer to the behaviour of minerals when affected by electricity, or to the ways

Fig. 6-7   Note the curved fractures on this damaged quartz crystal. It illustrates the typical conchoidal fracture of this mineral. The crystal comes from Minas Gerais, Brazil, and is about 5 cm. wide

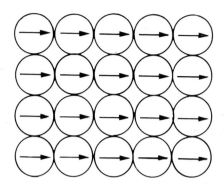

Fig. 6-8 Magnetite: the magnetism of the iron atoms reinforce one another

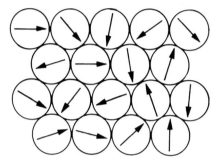

Hematite: the magnetism of the iron atoms cancel each other

in which minerals, under certain conditions, may produce electric currents. Most minerals are either conductors or non-conductors of electricity. Some non-conductors have the power to produce electricity when under pressure or when heated.

For practical purposes, the measurement and even the description of the electrical qualities of minerals require the use of sophisticated instruments. Some elements such as gold, silver and copper are good conductors of electricity; some sulphide minerals also are conductors. Quartz and tourmaline are non-conductors.

A conductor like copper has its atoms held together by forces called *metallic bonds*. This type of bond allows the continuous transfer of electrons from one atom to the next. Because of this process, electricity applied to one end of a specimen of copper can be carried right through the specimen. Good conductors are used to carry power from the source to the consumer.

Tourmaline crystals, when subjected to a temperature change, develop positive and negative charges at opposite ends of the crystal. This property is called *pyroelectricity*. In tourmaline crystals the temperature change causes the atoms in the structure to become unstable, and their attempts to regain stability produce opposite charges at the ends of the crystal. However, the amount of charge developed is very small and is difficult to detect. Quartz crystals produce an electric current when the crystal is pressed. This property is called *piezoelectricity*. Quartz crystals are composed of silicon and oxygen atoms. The arrangement is such that, if the crystal is squeezed or distorted, it disturbs this stable arrangement of atoms, and their attempt to regain stability produces electricity. The opposite also is true; if electricity is applied to quartz crystals, they will bend slightly. Thin wafers of quartz, cut from specially selected directions in a crystal, can be made to vibrate at a steady rate if an oscillating electrical current is applied. The rate of oscillation of the current determines the rate of vibration of the wafer. This property is used to make oscillator plates for radio transmitters, since suitable vibration frequencies can be produced by applying the proper current.

Radioactive Properties

Minerals that emit high energy radiation are said to be *radioactive*. The property depends on the presence of unstable atoms which are giving off radiation continuously in their effort to achieve a more stable state.

Although we know of various types of radiation such as alpha-rays, beta-rays and gamma-rays, advanced techniques are needed to distinguish between them. The presence of general radiation, however, can be detected and measured with various devices such as the scintillation counter.

Radioactive minerals possess this property because they contain radioactive elements such as atoms of uranium (in the mineral uraninite) and thorium (in the mineral thorite). Although many radioactive minerals are crystalline, others are metamict and have no orderly arrangement of atoms (see Chapter 3, page 48).

Radioactive materials are used widely as a source of energy, but the radiation which they give out is only a small part of what they contain. Ways have been devised to release part of this energy and to convert it into other kinds, such as heat, which can then be used to produce steam to drive turbines for the production of electricity.

Optical Properties

The optical properties of minerals also are physical in character and can be determined without the use of chemical means. Like the other properties, they are dependent upon the kinds and arrangements of atoms in the structures of the minerals. Generally, the optical properties are difficult to determine and to do so requires special equipment. The study of these properties is a wide field of its own and lies beyond the scope of this book.

With practice, the beginner can learn to measure or describe most of these properties for a given mineral, and thus be able to identify it. Identification tables are common in many mineralogy books and some are listed in the references at the end of this book. The principal use of the physical properties is to identify minerals relatively quickly and simply.

Fig. 6-9   This superb cleavage fragment of a gypsum crystal from the Kingdom Mine, Galetta, Ontario, Canada, is almost perfectly transparent. It measures 25 x 21 cm. and is about 3 cm. thick

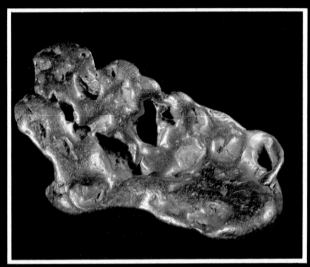

16

Plate 16   Gold nugget, California, U.S.A.

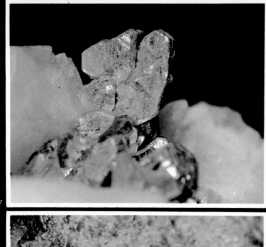

17

Plate 17 Gold crystals on white quartz. California, U.S.A.

Plate 18 Diamond crystal. Kimberley, Republic of South Africa

Plate 19 Sulphur crystals. Sicily.

Plate 20 Sphalerite crystals, dark reddish-brown. Switzerland

18

19

20

Plate 21   Hematite crystals. The long side of the picture represents about 4 cm. of the specimen. Brazil

Plate 22   Pyrite crystals. Colorado, U.S.A.

Plate 23   Halite. Poland

Plate 24   Purple fluorite crystals. England

Plate 25   Gypsum rosette. Manitoba, Canada

Plate 26   Barite. South Dakota, U.S.A.

Plate 27   Calcite. Michigan, U.S.A.

Plate 28   Apatite crystal. Quebec, Canada

Plate 29   Vanadinite. Morocco

27

28

29

Plate 30   Autunite. Washington, U.S.A.
Plate 31   Wulfenite. Arizona, U.S.A.
Plate 32   Grossular. Vermont, U.S.A.
Plate 33   Dioptase crystals. South West Africa
Plate 34   Zoisite crystal.Tanzania

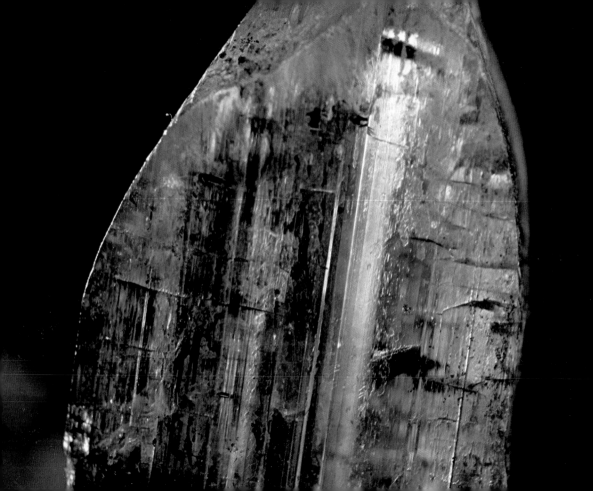

Plate 35   Hornblende crystal. Ontario, Canada

Plate 36   Apophyllite crystals. Poona, India

Plate 37   Quartz, variety amethyst. Mexico

Plate 38   Microcline, variety amazonite.
Colorado, U.S.A.

Non-Silicate Minerals: A Classification

As we have seen in previous chapters, most minerals are crystalline and they have definite chemical compositions. Although the chemical composition of a mineral may vary slightly, it can do so only within certain limits. Every crystalline mineral has a regular three-dimensional arrangement of atoms, which is called the crystal structure. Now we shall see that these two factors, chemistry and crystallography, are important in the systematic classification of minerals. This chapter describes the classification of the non-silicates (those minerals which do not contain silicon atoms as a main component), and the next chapter will be devoted to the classification of the silicate minerals (those minerals which do contain silicon atoms as a major component).

The Classification

The classification of minerals is one of the most important aspects of mineralogy. As in the case of the other natural sciences, we are concerned with finding an orderly scheme in the natural world.

Several attempts have been made to classify minerals. One classification is that of James Dwight Dana who, in 1857, proposed a scheme of grouping minerals. The original Dana System of Classification relied heavily upon the chemistry of minerals and also upon the outward shapes of their crystals (*morphological crystallography*). Since that time, the discovery, about 1912, that the crystal structures of minerals could be worked out by means of X-rays has modified the classification. The new Dana System, as revised by Charles Palache, Harry Berman and Clifford Frondel, is founded on the chemistry but is modified by the arrangements of atoms in the minerals of each group. By making such a classification, it is sometimes possible to predict chemical compositions and crystal structures which, as yet, have not been found at all.

In a small book such as this, it is not possible to list all the mineral groups of the Dana System, so only the main ones are given. Under each heading the chemical symbols of the elements and also the chemical compositions (chemical formulae) of the minerals are given in brackets.

NATIVE ELEMENTS

This group contains those minerals which are composed of only one kind of atom. It is the simplest of all the mineral divisions. Within the group the subdivisions are based partly on chemistry and partly on crystal structure. Some examples are: gold (Au), copper (Cu), sulphur (S), graphite (C) and diamond (C).

Gold Nugget, California, U.S.A. (Plate 16)

This magnificent gold nugget is sixteen centimetres long and averages about six centimetres high. Its size, shape and "warm" gold colour make it a fine specimen of this mineral. It is composed of gold atoms, which are scarce in the crust of the earth, and are rarely found in such large amounts. Gold is malleable and can be beaten out into very thin sheets to make gold leaf. Its specific gravity is about 19 (gold is a heavy atom). It usually contains other atoms as impurities, such as silver or copper atoms. These impurities may cause the colour to change to silvery-gold or coppery-gold. Its hardness is $1\frac{1}{2}$, and it has no cleavage.

This nugget is typically rounded as a result of having been washed about in a fast-flowing stream. The action of rolling in the river bed also has broken away much of the quartz which probably was associated with it.

Gold Crystals, California, U.S.A. (Plate 17)

Gold usually occurs as nuggets or fine, scattered grains; but we sometimes find crystals. These are rare and, like the ones in the photograph, usually imperfect. The gold atoms are arranged in a cubic repeat pattern, and the building blocks are stacked in such a way as to make an octahedron (see Fig. 10

in Chapter 2). The largest crystal in the photograph is triangular in shape, and is about seven millimetres (one millimetre equals one-tenth of a centimetre) along an edge. This crystal probably is part of a distorted octahedron and, although not perfect, the specimen is particularly fine and the crystals quite distinct.

Diamond, Kimberley, Republic of South Africa (Plate 18)

This diamond crystal is about seven millimetres across and is composed entirely of carbon atoms. The crystal is in the natural rock, kimberlite, in which it is formed (see Chapter 4, page 53). Diamonds are so rare that even in diamond mines they are not usually seen until the final stages of the recovery process. By this time the diamond crystals have been separated from the rock and so a specimen like this, with the diamond crystal actually in place in the kimberlite, is a great rarity. Diamond crystallizes in the cubic crystal system, and usually the crystals have rounded faces (like the one shown here). Its hardness is 10 and specific gravity about 3.5. Diamonds are prized for their physical properties; because of their brilliance, hardness and rarity, they are used as gemstones; for industrial purposes they are set into cutting tools which can cut and polish almost any known material.

Sulphur, Sicily, Italy (Plate 19)

This beautifully shaped specimen is highlighted by a large crystal which is 3×3 centimetres square. The sharpness of this crystal adds to the interest of the specimen. The mineral is composed of sulphur atoms (S) and is used in various chemical processes. Sharp, spectacular crystals such as these are not common, the usual form being indistinct masses. Sulphur crystals have orthorhombic symmetry, poor cleavage, are brittle and have a greasy or resinous lustre. Its hardness is $1\frac{1}{2}$ to $2\frac{1}{2}$ and sulphur has a specific gravity of about 2. In perfect crystals it is transparent, but usually it is translucent.

SULPHIDES (This group also includes arsenides, bismuthinides, antimonides, tellurides and selenides.)

These minerals are nearly all metallic in appearance and are composed of various elements combined with one of the following: sulphur (S), arsenic (As), bismuth (Bi), antimony (Sb), tellurium (Te) or selenium (Se). Galena (PbS) is composed of lead (Pb) and sulphur (S)—see Fig. 2-5 of the crystal structure model and specimen. Sphalerite (ZnS) and pyrite (FeS_2) also are sulphide minerals. Some others are: calaverite ($AuTe_2$), a gold telluride; sperrylite ($PtAs_2$), a platinum arsenide; and arsenopyrite (FeAsS), an iron arsenide-sulphide.

Galena Crystals, Japan (Plate 2)

The galena crystals shown here are much more perfect than those in Fig. 2-5. These one-centimetre crystals are cube-shaped, but notice that some of them appear to have their corners cut off. This is the effect of the combination of two crystal forms (shapes), the cube and the octahedron (see Fig. 2-11). The cube faces develop as a result of the prominent planes of atoms at right angles to each other in the crystal structure; the octahedral faces develop parallel to other prominent planes of atoms which are at an angle to the cube planes. Galena has three perfect cleavage directions which are parallel to the sides of the cube. The mineral is metallic, has a lead-grey colour, hardness about $2\frac{1}{2}$ and specific gravity $7\frac{1}{2}$ (due to the heavy lead atom).

Sphalerite, Switzerland (Plate 20)

Sphalerite is composed of zinc (Zn) and sulphur (S) atoms in equal numbers. The chemical composition is therefore ZnS. These crystals are about ten millimetres high. They are accentuated by the white background of quartz and albite. These crystals have cubic symmetry, but the crystal forms (shapes) are quite complex. Sphalerite has six directions of perfect cleavage; its lustre is usually resinous; it varies in colour from yellow to black, although some specimens may be ruby-red. Its hardness is about $3\frac{1}{2}$ and its specific gravity is about 4. The mineral is the main ore of zinc.

Pyrite, Colorado, U.S.A. (Plate 22)

Pyrite is composed of iron (Fe) and sulphur (S) atoms; there is one iron atom for every two sulphur atoms; therefore its chemical composition is FeS_2. Pyrite is probably the most common sulphide and may be found in a variety of different types of rocks. It crystallizes with cubic symmetry and the crystals may be large and have perfect mirror-like faces. The ones shown here are cubes, about two centimetres along each edge. The metallic pyrite shows clearly against the white quartz crystals. It has no distinct cleavage, is usually brassy-yellow in colour and is brittle. Its hardness is about 6 and its specific gravity close to 5.

SULPHOSALTS

The sulphosalts are similar to the sulphides in appearance, being mainly metallic minerals. They are composed of elements combined with sulphur and, in addition, one or all of the following: arsenic (As), bismuth (Bi), antimony (Sb) and tin (Sn). There are more than 85 minerals in this group, and they are subdivided again on the basis of their chemistry and crystal structures. Proustite (Ag_3AsS_3), a silver-arsenic sulphide, is an example. This mineral is unusual in that perfect crystals are transparent and ruby-red in colour. Sulphosalts generally are quite rare, metallic, grey in colour, and occur only in small quantities.

OXIDES AND HYDROXIDES

This group is also quite large, and contains minerals which are composed of elements combined with oxygen or hydrogen and oxygen. However, we exclude the silicate minerals, which are composed of elements combined with silicon and oxygen atoms, as these form several groups of their own (see Chapter 8). Ilmenite is an example of an oxide; it is composed of iron (Fe), titanium (Ti) and oxygen (O) atoms, one iron plus one titanium plus three oxygens, giving the chemical formula $FeTiO_3$. Uraninite (UO_2), is a uranium oxide; hematite (Fe_2O_3), is an iron oxide; goethite ($HFeO_2$), is a hydrogen iron oxide; chrysoberyl ($BeAl_2O_4$), is an oxide of beryllium (Be) and aluminum (Al).

Hematite Crystals, Brazil (Plate 21)

The crystals shown here represent only about four centimetres of this magnificent specimen (measured along the long side of the picture). It

was chosen to show the spectacular crystals of this oxide of iron. The chemistry involves atoms of iron (Fe) and oxygen (O), two iron atoms for every three oxygens, Fe_2O_3. This mineral is a common ore of iron. Usually it is found as fine-grained, red, dusty masses; or as rounded, shiny, kidney-shaped (reniform) masses (Fig. 7-1). It is only rarely found as brilliant crystals.

The crystal system of hematite is hexagonal; we can see the three-fold symmetry of the triangular patterns on the crystal faces. Notice that even the faintest of these growth lines on the faces conforms to the regular triangular pattern—a further testimony to the orderly arrangement of atoms within the crystals.

Some physical properties of hematite are: metallic lustre; hardness, 5-6; specific gravity, 5.2; no cleavage; colour of the streak (powder), cherry-red.

HALIDES

These minerals are composed of elements combined with any of the following: fluorine (F), chlorine (Cl), bromine (Br) or iodine (I). Some examples are: fluorite, (CaF_2), a calcium fluoride, well known for its beautiful colours and sharp cubic crystals; halite (NaCl) is a chloride of sodium (Na), familiar to us as common table salt.

Halite, Poland (Plate 23)

Halite crystallizes in the cubic crystal system. The crystals in this picture are cubes, about $3\frac{1}{2}$ centimetres along the edges. The chemistry involves atoms of sodium (Na) and chlorine (Cl) in equal numbers. The chemical formula is therefore NaCl.

These beautiful crystals, well formed, with sharp edges, were selected for their perfection rather than their size. The arrangement of atoms in halite is the same as the arrangement of atoms in galena (though different atoms are involved). Halite, like galena, has three directions of perfect cleavage parallel to the faces of the cubic crystals. This is because both minerals have the same arrangements of atoms.

The hardness of halite is 2; it is brittle; its lustre is vitreous (glassy); specific gravity is just over 2, and its taste is salty.

Fig. 7-1   Hematite or "kidney ore" from Cumberland, England. The specimen is 9 x 6 cm.

Fig. 7-2   A magnificent twinned cerussite specimen. Each crystal is about 10 x 10 x 2½ cm. It is from Tsumeb, South West Africa

Fluorite, England (Plate 24)

The picture shows some fine single cubic crystals and also some twinned crystals of fluorite. The latter are formed by the intergrowth of two cubes. Fluorite is a beautiful mineral, varying widely in colour and frequently crystallizing into large, sharp-edged crystals. The deep purple variety is the most common.

The elements present are calcium (Ca) and fluorine (F), with twice as many fluorine atoms as calcium atoms. The chemical formula is CaF_2. The four directions of perfect cleavage are parallel to the faces of an octahedron. Its hardness is 4; specific gravity 3.1; its colour varies—colourless, yellow, green, blue, violet, purple, pink, white, grey. When exposed to ultraviolet light, most specimens of fluorite fluoresce bluish-white.

The faces of the crystals shown in the photograph are interesting as they show traces of their lines of growth.

CARBONATES

The minerals in this division are composed of elements combined with the carbonate group (CO_3) (Fig. 7-2). Some of the minerals are quite simple, such as calcite ($CaCO_3$), a calcium carbonate. Others are more complex like hydromagnesite [$Mg_4(CO_3)_3(OH)_2.3H_2O$]. Malachite [$Cu_2(CO_3)(OH)_2$] and azurite [$Cu_3(CO_3)_2(OH)_2$] are both carbonate-hydroxides of copper (Cu) and are brilliantly coloured; malachite green, and azurite blue.

Calcite, Michigan, U.S.A. (Plate 27)

This clear, colourless crystal of calcite is a superb example; it is about $4\frac{1}{2}$ centimetres high and grew on top of a plate of native copper. Some of the pinkish crystals in the foreground are calcite which contain some copper crystals which cause their colour (see Plate 10). The many faces on this specimen indicate the complexity of this crystal. Its symmetry places it in the hexagonal system. It is possible to see completely through this transparent crystal. If you look carefully at the picture, you will see that everything behind the crystal is doubled. This is one of the special optical properties of this mineral.

96

Several other pictures of calcite are in this book, and most of them are described in detail. See Fig 6-6, Plates 9 and 10.

Calcite is composed of calcium (Ca) atoms, together with the carbonate group of atoms (CO_3). In calcite, one calcium matches one carbonate group; the chemical formula is therefore $CaCO_3$. The (CO_3) combination of atoms characterizes all of the carbonate group of minerals.

Some of the physical properties of calcite are: three directions of perfect cleavage not at right angles to each other; hardness 3; specific gravity about 3; lustre vitreous or sometimes pearly on cleavage faces. The colour is variable: colourless, white, yellow, brown, pink, blue, green, grey and black. However, the colour of the streak (powder) is white, regardless of the colour of the specimen.

Dolomite, Spain (Plate 3)

Dolomite is another carbonate mineral. It is composed of atoms of calcium (Ca) and magnesium (Mg) with the carbonate group (CO_3). There is a carbonate group for each calcium atom, and one for each magnesium atom. The chemical formula is therefore $CaCO_3.MgCO_3$ which usually is written $CaMg(CO_3)_2$. The crystal in the picture is twinned, and the two parts of the twin are remarkably clear and perfect for this mineral. The specimen is about three centimetres high. Some physical properties are: three perfect directions of cleavage which are not at right angles; hardness $3\frac{1}{2}$-4; specific gravity about 3; lustre vitreous to pearly; colour white, colourless, brown or pink.

Malachite, Arizona, U.S.A. (Plate 5)

Malachite is an ore of copper. Its green colour is typical and varies very little. Crystals are rare and usually are shaped like fine needles. Malachite often forms rounded, bumpy masses called botryoidal aggregates (see Chapter 3, page 45). The picture shows a polished slice through a botryoidal specimen and shows the rings, which are sections cut through the rounded bumps. Each of the bumps is composed of fine-grained aggregates of needle-like crystals radiating out from a centre. This polished specimen, about ten centimetres long, is amusing as the pattern suggests a pair of eyes and a nose.

The chemistry is rather complex, consisting of copper atoms (Cu), with the carbonate group (CO_3) and also the hydroxyl group (OH). The latter is made of one hydrogen and one oxygen atom. The proportions are: two coppers, one carbonate group and two hydroxyl groups, to give the chemical formula $Cu_2(CO_3)(OH)_2$.

Some physical properties are: hardness $3\frac{1}{4}$-4; specific gravity about 4; translucent to opaque; colour, bright green.

NITRATES

Nitrates are a small group of minerals composed of elements combined with the nitrate group (NO_3). An example is nitre $K(NO_3)$, a nitrate of potassium (K).

BORATES

Borates are minerals that contain elements combined with one of the borate groups. There are several of these groups, each containing various proportions of boron (B) and oxygen (O). An example is the mineral borax, $Na_2B_4O_7.10H_2O$, a sodium (Na) borate which contains water molecules (H_2O).

SULPHATES

This is a large group of minerals which are composed of various elements combined with the sulphate group (SO_4). Celestite, $SrSO_4$, a strontium sulphate, is one. Gypsum ($CaSO_4.2H_2O$) is a hydrated calcium sulphate. There are many other mineral species in this group, and all are subdivided on the basis of their chemistry and crystal structure. Some of them have very complex chemical compositions.

Barite, South Dakota, U.S.A. (Plate 26)

This lovely crystal of golden barite is $4\frac{1}{2}$ centimetres high. Its clarity and colour are unusual for this mineral, as well as its shape. It is composed of atoms of barium (Ba) and the sulphate group of atoms (SO_4). The latter consists of one sulphur (S) and four oxygens (O). Thus the chemical composition or formula of barite is $BaSO_4$.

The small yellow crystals in the background are calcite, a fine colour to show off the deep golden

colour of the barite. This specimen is specially attractive for this reason, though barite itself is not a rare mineral.

Some physical properties are: the crystal symmetry is orthorhombic; it has one perfect cleavage direction; hardness $3-3\frac{1}{2}$; specific gravity $4\frac{1}{2}$ (due to the heavy barium atom); its lustre is vitreous or resinous, but sometimes pearly. Colour varies: white, colourless, shades of yellow and brown, blue and green.

Gypsum, Manitoba, Canada (Plate 25)

In this specimen of gypsum, a number of crystals have grown together, each originating at the centre of the group, to make this beautiful rosette. The whole specimen is $7\frac{1}{2}$ centimetres high. The crystals are pale yellow and transparent. The atoms in the structure are calcium (Ca) and the sulphate group (SO_4), combined with two molecules of water (H_2O). The chemical formula is $CaSO_4.2H_2O$.

Some of its physical properties are: one perfect cleavage direction; flexible, meaning that thin plates can be bent, but are not elastic; they remain bent when the bending force is removed. Hardness is 2; specific gravity is 2.3; lustre is sub-vitreous, but pearly on cleavage faces; colour can be white, colourless, yellow, brown or grey. (See also Fig. 7-3.)

CHROMATES

The minerals belonging to this small group are composed of various elements combined with a chromate group, either CrO_4 or Cr_2O_7. An example is crocoite, a bright orange-red mineral, which is a lead (Pb) chromate.

PHOSPHATES, ARSENATES AND VANADATES

This is a large group of minerals and generally consists of various elements combined with either the phosphate group (PO_4), or elements combined with the arsenate group (AsO_4), or elements combined with the vanadate group (VO_4). The three main groups—phosphates, arsenates and vanadates—are placed together in one major division. Triphylite, $LiFe(PO_4)$, is a lithium (Li) iron (Fe) phosphate. Apatite [$Ca_5(PO_4)_3(F,Cl)$], is a common phosphate composed of calcium phosphate with fluorine (F) and/or chlorine (Cl).

Fig. 7-3 Slender crystals of gypsum about 3 cm. long. The specimen is from Crystal Falls, Michigan

Erythrite [$Co_3(AsO_4)_2.8H_2O$] is a cobalt (Co) arsenate with eight water molecules (H_2O). Descloisite [$ZnPb(VO)_4(OH)$] is a basic zinc (Zn) lead (Pb) vanadate (Fig. 7-4). Vanadinite [$Pb_5(VO_4)_3Cl$] is a vanadate of lead (Pb) with chlorine (Cl). These examples are given here to show the variety and complexity of this group.

Apatite, Quebec, Canada (Plate 28)

Apatite has hexagonal symmetry and frequently shows six-sided crystals. In this picture only two of the six sides are showing, the others are embedded in orange calcite. The crystal is seven centimetres long. Its chemistry is complex, but essentially it is composed of calcium atoms (Ca) with the phosphate group which consists of one phosphorous atom and four oxygens (PO_4). Other atoms, such as fluorine (F), chlorine (Cl), hydrogen and oxygen (OH), may enter into the structure.

Physical properties are: no good cleavage; hardness 5; specific gravity 3.1; lustre vitreous to resinous; colour green, blue, yellow-green, blue-green, violet, red, white or colourless.

Vanadinite, Morocco (Plate 29)

Crystals of vanadinite have hexagonal symmetry; many of the crystals shown here have six sides. These crystals are sharp and well formed, also evenly spaced on the rock, and make an attractive mineral specimen. The long side of the picture represents about four centimetres of the specimen.

The chemistry of vanadinite involves atoms of lead (Pb), combined with the vanadate group (VO_4) and atoms of chlorine (Cl). Five lead atoms combine with three vanadate groups and one chlorine atom, giving a chemical formula $Pb_5(VO_4)_3Cl$.

Some physical properties of vanadinite are: no cleavage; hardness about 3; specific gravity $6\frac{1}{2}$-7 (due to the heavy lead and vanadium atoms); lustre sub-resinous to brilliant; colour, various shades of red, also brown and yellow.

Autunite, Washington, U.S.A. (Plate 30)

This picture shows the typical sheaf-like aggregates of autunite crystals. The long side of the picture represents about 14 centimetres of the specimen. The mineral is rare in such large quantities, and this specimen is particularly excellent.

The chemistry is complex, involving atoms of calcium (Ca) with groups of atoms composed of one uranium atom (U) and two oxygens (O), as well as the phosphate group (PO_4) and water molecules (H_2O). One calcium atom combines with two UO_2 groups, two PO_4 groups and between 10 and 12 water molecules. The chemical formula may be written $Ca(UO_2)_2(PO_4)_2.10\text{-}12H_2O$.

Some of the physical properties of autunite are: one perfect cleavage direction; hardness $2\text{-}2\frac{1}{2}$; specific gravity 3.1; lustre vitreous (pearly on cleavage faces); colour is lemon yellow, various shades of green. It gives a strong yellow-green fluorescence under ultraviolet light and is transparent or translucent.

MOLYBDATES AND TUNGSTATES

Minerals of these groups are composed of elements combined with either the molybdate group (MoO_4) or the tungstate group (WO_4). Wulfenite ($PbMoO_4$) is a lead (Pb) molybdate which often shows superb development of crystal forms. Scheelite ($CaWO_4$) is a calcium (Ca) tungstate.

Wulfenite, Arizona, U.S.A. (Plate 31)

These crystals belong to the tetragonal crystal system. They are thin and translucent. Wulfenite varies in colour; shades of yellow and brown are common, but some specimens are red and others are green. Although many specimens show crystals that are paper-thin, others have thick, blocky crystals.

The chemistry involves atoms of lead (Pb) combined with the molybdate group, composed of one molybdenum atom (Mo) with four oxygen atoms, to give MoO_4. One lead atom combines with one molybdate group to give the chemical formula $PbMoO_4$.

Some physical properties are: one distinct cleavage direction; hardness about 3; specific gravity $6\frac{1}{2}\text{-}7$ (due to the heavy lead and molybdenum atoms); lustre resinous to brilliant; colour variable, but the streak (powder) is white.

Fig. 7-4 This attractive crystal group of the mineral descloisite comes from Berg Aukas, South West Africa, and is about 6 x 4½ cm.

101

Silicate Minerals: A Classification

We have seen that minerals can be conveniently divided into two major groups: those which contain silicon and oxygen (the silicates) and those which do not (the non-silicates). In this chapter we shall deal exclusively with the silicate minerals, and we shall see that their classification is based on the ways in which the silicon and oxygen atoms are arranged. The chemistry of the silicate minerals plays a lesser role in the classification scheme.

The silicate minerals comprise a large and rather complex group. They are composed of various kinds of atoms combined with one or more of the silicate groups. These groups are made up of various proportions of silicon atoms (Si) and oxygen atoms (O). Quartz, hornblende, topaz and beryl are examples of silicate minerals, as well as the Mica Group of minerals, the Garnet Group and the Tourmaline Group.

The Silicon-Oxygen Tetrahedron, The Basic Unit of All Silicate Minerals

The basic unit in the structures of all silicate minerals is the silicon-oxygen tetrahedron; it is composed of one atom of silicon and four atoms of oxygen (SiO_4). It is illustrated in Fig. 8-1, and we can see that there are three oxygen atoms, which make a triangle, and that the silicon atom fits into the centre of these three. The fourth oxygen atom is placed directly on top of the silicon atom, so that the silicon atom is completely surrounded by the four oxygen atoms. This sketch represents a silicon-oxygen tetrahedron as it would be in an actual mineral structure; all four oxygen atoms

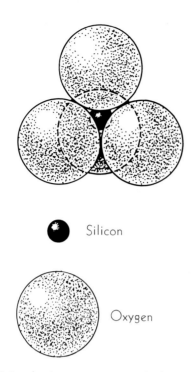

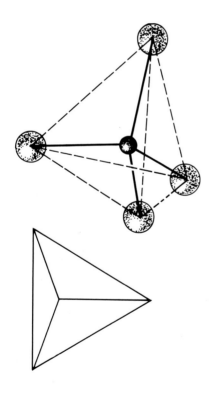

● Silicon

Oxygen

Fig. 8-1   A silicon-oxygen tetrahedron

Fig. 8-2   An expanded view and a diagrammatic
sketch of a silicon-oxygen tetrahedron

are touching each other, and also each one touches the silicon atom. Fig. 8-2 shows the same silicon-oxygen tetrahedron expanded, with the atoms placed further apart so that the arrangement can be seen more clearly. The basic shape is outlined, and this is like a three-sided pyramid, and is called a tetrahedron. The word *tetrahedron* means a four-sided shape, the three sides of the pyramid plus the base. The expanded sketch of the silicon-oxygen tetrahedron is a bit misleading because the size of the oxygen atom, compared with the silicon atom, is not correct. In fact, the silicon atom is much smaller than the oxygen atom. Most drawings of mineral structures, however, use the expanded style of illustration because the structure can be seen more clearly. In actual mineral structures, the atoms are as close together as possible and usually touch one another.

The chemical formula of the basic silicate unit is SiO_4, meaning four oxygens associated with one silicon atom. However, there are various ways in which these silicon-oxygen groups can be joined together, and we shall see in the next few pages that varying proportions of silicon to oxygen are possible in silicate minerals. These proportions are dependent upon the ways in which the tetrahedra are joined to one another.

A further complication arises in the silicate minerals because of the aluminum atom. This atom is similar in size and chemical nature to the silicon atom, and therefore it can occupy an oxygen tetrahedron in place of a silicon atom. Therefore the aluminum tetrahedron (AlO_4) is very similar in size to the silicon-oxygen tetrahedron (SiO_4) and so can enter into any one of the possible tetrahedral arrangements in silicate structures. Minerals which contain silicon-oxygen and aluminum-oxygen tetrahedral units are properly called alumino-silicates. Muscovite, the Feldspar Group of minerals and the Zeolite Group are examples of alumino-silicates. We shall call them simply "silicate minerals."

Independent Tetrahedra in a Mineral Structure

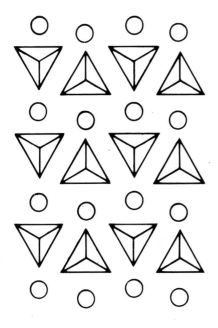

SiO₄ tetrahedron

◯ Other atoms in the structure

Fig. 8-3   Independent SiO₄ tetrahedra in a mineral structure

atoms which hold together silicon-oxygen tetrahedra, but the tetrahedra are not joined to one another. Because of this, the "SiO" part of the chemical formula of all the minerals in this group is SiO_4. Fig. 8-3 shows how this is possible, but the sketch is diagrammatic and does not represent an actual mineral structure. The structures of most of the silicate minerals are too complex to illustrate and only diagrams are used here. Some examples of minerals in this silicate group are: the Olivine Group, in which iron and magnesium atoms hold together the SiO_4 groups so that their general formula is $(Fe,Mg)SiO_4$; the Garnet Group of minerals (also nesosilicates) are more complex, and one of these minerals is described below in more detail and illustrated in Plate 32.

Grossular Crystals, a Nesosilicate Mineral (Plate 32)

The red grossular crystals shown in this picture are the common isometric crystal form called the rhombic dodecahedron. Each crystal has twelve faces, each of which is the same size and shape. The crystals are nearly of gem quality, being quite clear and of pleasing colour. They are flawed, however, by internal fractures. Each of these crystals is about five millimetres along each edge.

Grossular is a mineral species belonging to the Garnet Group. It is a nesosilicate, and so contains independent groups of silicon and oxygen atoms in tetrahedral arrangements. The chemical formula must have SiO_4 as a part of it, regardless of the other kinds of atoms present. In grossular, atoms of calcium and aluminum hold together the SiO_4 tetrahedra. Three calcium atoms and two aluminum atoms combine with three groups of SiO_4 to make the formula $Ca_3Al_2(SiO_4)_3$. Note that $(SiO_4)_3$ is the same as Si_3O_{12} or $3(SiO_4)$.

Garnet Group minerals are common in the rocks of the earth, and all have atomic arrangements which are essentially similar to the one described for grossular. In the other minerals of the group other atoms are involved, but the Si-O part of the formula remains the same: for example, almandine $[Fe_3Al_2(SiO_4)_3]$, an iron aluminum silicate; pyrope $[Mg_3Al_2(SiO_4)_3]$, a magnesium aluminum silicate; and the dark green garnet, uvarovite

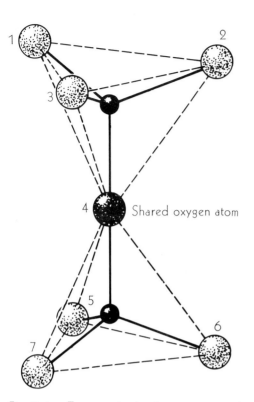

[Ca₃Cr₂(SiO₄)₃], a calcium chromium silicate.

Some of the physical properties of grossular are: no cleavage; hardness 6½ to 7; specific gravity about 3.5; colour variable—green, white, pink, brown, red or orange.

Double Tetrahedra in a Mineral Structure

In minerals belonging to this group, the silicate part of the structure is characterized by pairs of SiO_4 tetrahedra linked together. The two tetrahedra share one of the oxygen atoms and so there are two silicon atoms and seven oxygen atoms (Si_2O_7).

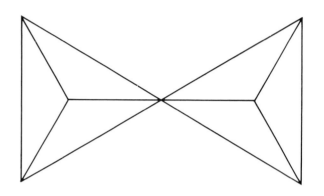

Fig. 8-4a Two tetrahedra sharing one oxygen (Si_2O_7): an expanded view and a diagrammatic sketch

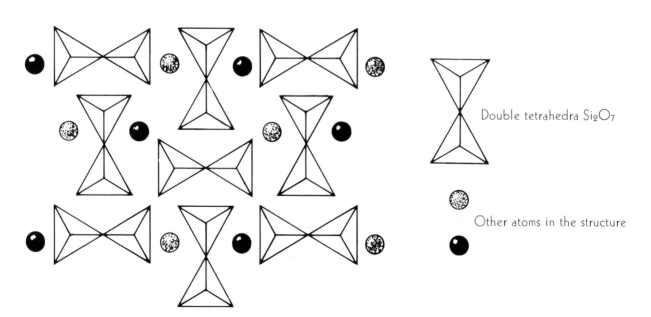

Double tetrahedra Si_2O_7

Other atoms in the structure

Fig. 8-4b Double tetrahedra in a mineral structure

(See Fig. 8-4a, in which there are seven oxygens.) The technical name for this group is the *sorosilicates*. Each pair of linked silicon-oxygen tetrahedra are held together in the structure by other kinds of atoms. Fig. 8-4b shows a very simplified diagram of a structure containing pairs of tetrahedra. Epidote is a common mineral which belongs to this group of silicate minerals. Its chemistry and structure are complex, but the formula does contain Si_2O_7 groups. In addition, however, it contains some independent tetrahedra-SiO_4, and is therefore a mixed type of silicate containing both the nesosilicate and sorosilicate types.

A Zoisite Crystal, a Sorosilicate Mineral (Plate 34)

The fine crystal shown in this picture is from Tanzania. It is a crystal of the unusual and newly discovered (1967) gem variety of the mineral zoisite. It has orthorhombic symmetry and is about $2\frac{1}{2}$ centimetres high. The brilliant, clear blue colour, tipped with pale yellow, is unusual for specimens of this mineral. At present these are known only from Tanzania. This crystal is not good enough to be used as a gemstone, but still it makes a fine mineral specimen. Other crystals of excellent gem quality have been found and have been cut into spectacular gemstones.

The chemistry of zoisite is quite complex, but the essential character of the structure is shown by the presence of the Si_2O_7 groups. The classification of zoisite into the sorosilicate group is complicated by the fact that it contains some of the independent tetrahedra SiO_4 as well. The silicon-oxygen groups are held together in the structure by atoms of calcium, aluminum and the oxygen-hydrogen group (OH).

Some physical properties of zoisite are: one perfect cleavage direction; hardness 6; specific gravity 3.2; colour grey, green, brown, pink and blue.

A Note About Nesosilicates and Sorosilicates

Some classification schemes for the silicate minerals place both these groups together. The combined

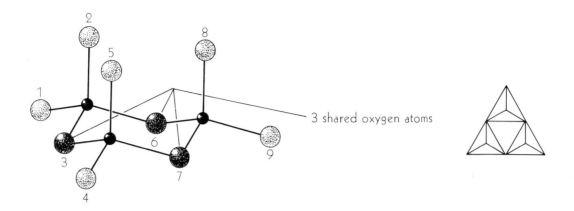

Fig. 8-5a   Three-fold ring of tetrahedra Si_3O_9 with a diagrammatic view

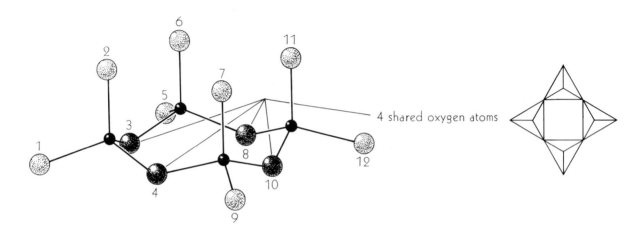

Fig. 8-5b   Four-fold ring of tetrahedra Si_4O_{12} with a diagrammatic view

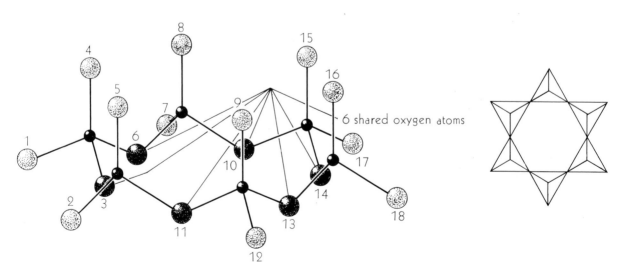

Fig. 8-5c   Six-fold ring of tetrahedra Si_6O_{18} with diagrammatic view

108

group is called the Orthosilicate Group and these are characterized by the presence of independent SiO_4 groups or independent Si_2O_7 groups, or a combination of both.

Rings of Tetrahedra in a Mineral Structure

In these silicates, the SiO_4 tetrahedra are linked to each other to make rings. The group is sometimes called the *cyclosilicates*. They may form rings of three, four or six tetrahedral groups. Because the SiO_4 tetrahedra which make the rings are joined to one another by sharing an oxygen atom between each successive pair, the characteristic parts of the formulae are not simply multiples of SiO_4.

The proportions of silicon to oxygen atoms in each case are:

Three-fold ring Si_3O_9 (three oxygens are shared).
Four-fold ring Si_4O_{12} (four oxygens are shared).
Six-fold ring Si_6O_{18} (six oxygens are shared).

In the diagrams in Fig. 8-5a, b and c, these three types of silicate rings are shown.

In the various crystal structures of different materials belonging to this group of silicates other kinds of atoms may be held together by the rings of silicon-oxygen tetrahedra.

Dioptase, a Ring Silicate Mineral (Plate 33)

Dioptase is a rather rare copper mineral which is characterized by six-fold rings of silicon-oxygen tetrahedra. Its distinctive dark green colour is also characteristic. The white quartz which makes up the background in this picture shows these crystals of dioptase to their best advantage. Dioptase occurs in only a few localities in the world, this specimen being from Tsumeb, South West Africa. The largest crystal in this group is about $1\frac{1}{2}$ centimetres long and, like all crystals of this mineral, has hexagonal symmetry.

The chemical formula of dioptase is characterized by Si_6O_{18} groups which represent the six-fold ring of tetrahedra. Other atoms which are holding these rings together are copper (Cu) and water molecules (H_2O). The chemical formula of dioptase is $Cu_6Si_6O_{18}.6H_2O$.

Some physical properites are: perfect rhombohedral cleavage (three directions not at

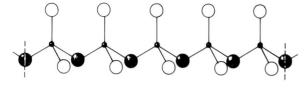

- • Silicon atoms
- ○ Unshared oxygens
- ● Shared oxygens

Fig. 8-6   Expanded and diagrammatic views of single chain of tetrahedra SiO_3

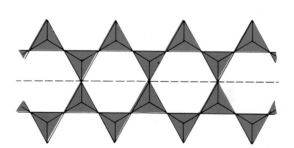

Fig. 8-7   Diagrammatic view of a double chain of tetrahedra

right angles, as in calcite); hardness 5; specific gravity about 3; colour, dark green.

Chains of Tetrahedra in a Mineral Structure

The silicon-oxygen tetrahedra in minerals belonging to this silicate group are joined into continuous chains. This silicate group sometimes is called the *inosilicates*. Fig. 8-6 shows diagrams of a single chain. These single chain-type minerals are characterized by SiO_3 groups, since each tetrahedron shares two of its oxygen atoms with the two tetrahedra on either side of it. The Pyroxene Group have chains of tetrahedra in their structures; the chains are held together in the structure by other kinds of atoms. Enstatite, a Pyroxene Group mineral, has the formula $(Mg,Fe)SiO_3$—a magnesium iron silicate; diopside is another Pyroxene Group mineral and has the formula $Ca(Mg,Fe)(SiO_3)_2$—a calcium magnesium iron silicate.

In some minerals belonging to this group, two single chains combine to form continuous double chains of tetrahedra. A double chain is represented in Fig. 8-7 and it can be seen that the alternating tetrahedra share first two oxygen atoms and then three oxygens with the neighbouring tetrahedra along the chain. This results in a formula of Si_4O_{11} for the double chain. This double chain is difficult to illustrate and only a diagrammatic view is shown in Fig. 8-7. Examples of minerals which have double chains in their structures are the members of the Amphibole Group. Hornblende is an amphibole mineral, and has a very complex crystal structure and chemical composition. The double chains in the structure of hornblende are held together by several other kinds of atoms; some of these are sodium (Na), calcium (Ca), potassium (K), iron (Fe), magnesium (Mg) and aluminum (Al). The silicate part of the formula, however, is ideally $(Si_4O_{11})_2$ which may be written as Si_8O_{22}. In the actual formula of hornblende some aluminum may be present in the tetrahedral groups and so the characteristic part of the formula should be $(Si,Al)_2O_{22}$. This means that there are eight atoms, some silicon and some aluminum which are combined with 22 atoms of oxygen. Hornblende is

110

illustrated in Plate 35, which is described below

A Hornblende Crystal, a Double Chain Silicate (Plate 35)

This black crystal of hornblende is only $1\frac{1}{2}$ centimetres long, but it is well formed and stands out against the pink calcite in which it is partly embedded. Hornblende crystals may reach large sizes, up to several feet in length.

The chemistry of hornblende is described briefly above and is too complex to discuss in any further detail.

Some physical properties are: two good cleavage directions at about 120 degrees to one another (see cleavage section in Chapter 6, which compares the cleavages of the Pyroxene Group and the Amphibole Group of minerals); hardness between 5 and 6; specific gravity about 3; colour green, brown or black.

Sheets of Tetrahedra in a Mineral Structure

In minerals which belong to this group of silicates, the structures are characterized by continuous sheets of silicon-oxygen tetrahedra. This group sometimes is called the *phyllosilicates*. The tetrahedra are joined together in such a way that each of the three oxygen atoms at the base of each tetrahedron is shared with another tetrahedron. Therefore every tetrahedron shares three of its four oxygen atoms, leaving only one unshared (see Fig. 8-8). The proportion of silicon atoms to oxygen atoms is Si_4O_{10}. The sheets of tetrahedra are held together by other types of atoms. The silicon-oxygen tetrahedral sheet is quite strong compared to the forces which hold the sheets together. Because of this, nearly all the minerals in the sheet silicate group have a perfect cleavage direction parallel to the sheets of tetrahedra. Minerals belonging to the Mica Group and the Serpentine Group (for example, chrysotile) are examples of this type of silicate.

Muscovite Crystals, a Sheet Silicate (Plate 6)

This fine group of muscovite crystals is about six centimetres high and is specially attractive because of the arrangement of the crystals. Its platy nature is a direct consequence of the arrangement of atoms in its crystal structure, which is illustrated in a simple diagrammatic version in Fig. 8-9. The

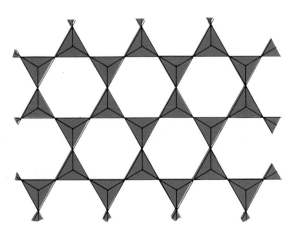

Fig. 8-8   Diagrammatic view of a continuous chain of tetrahedra

111

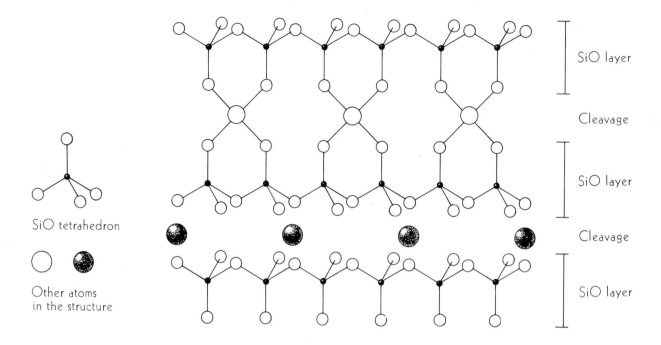

SiO tetrahedron

Other atoms
in the structure

Fig. 8-9   A diagrammatic view of a sheet-type structure

SiO layer

Cleavage

SiO layer

Cleavage

SiO layer

basic sheets of silicon and oxygen tetrahedra are joined together by other atoms in the structure, but these joins are weak compared to the strength of the silicon-oxygen sheet, therefore the crystals may be split between these sheets of tetrahedra. The cleavage is so perfect that sheets of muscovite thinner than a piece of paper can be peeled off with ease.

The silicate part of the chemical formula is ideally Si_4O_{10}, but these units may include some aluminum atoms and may be written Si_3AlO_{10}. In muscovite this unit is doubled and becomes $Si_6Al_2O_{20}$. The other atoms, the ones which hold the sheets together, are potassium (K), aluminum (Al), fluorine (F) and the oxygen-hydrogen group (OH). The formula is quite complex: $K_2Al_4(Si_6Al_2O_{20})(OH,F)_4$. The silicon, aluminum and oxygen atoms which make up the continuous sheet are enclosed in brackets $(Si_6Al_2O_{20})$; the other aluminum atoms in the formula are not part of the tetrahedra in the sheet.

Some physical properties are: one perfect cleavage direction parallel to the tetrahedral sheet; hardness $2\frac{1}{2}$ to 3; specific gravity about 2.8; variable colour but usually colourless or white, also pale shades of green, pink or brown.

112

Apophyllite Crystals, Another Sheet Silicate (Plate 36)

This specimen is especially beautiful, and the crystals are pale green in colour which is unusual for apophyllite. Most crystals of this mineral are white or colourless. Like muscovite, the silicate part of the chemical formula is Si_4O_{10}, but is doubled to Si_8O_{20}. Although the platy structure of this mineral is not as apparent as in muscovite, it does possess one perfect cleavage direction.

A Framework of Silicon-Oxygen Tetrahedra in a Mineral Structure

The technical name given to minerals of this group is *tektosilicates*. They are made up of three-dimensional networks of silicon-oxygen tetrahedra, each of which share all four oxygens with four other tetrahedra. Another way to describe the framework of tetrahedra is to say that every oxygen is shared by two tetrahedra. Therefore, the silicate part of the formula is SiO_2, one silicon atom plus four "half oxygen atoms." (Each of the four oxygens is shared between two tetrahedra.) Multiples of SiO_2 are permitted, such as Si_3O_6 or Si_4O_8. Quartz is a common mineral which is a framework silicate (Plate 8). Ideally, it is made up entirely of a network of silicon-oxygen tetrahedra and so its chemical composition is simply SiO_2; ideally, no other atoms are in the structure. The Feldspar Group of minerals also is composed of framework silicates, but the arrangement is less compact than that of quartz. Because of this, other atoms may enter into the structure.

Quartz Variety Amethyst, a Framework Silicate (Plate 37)

This very attractive group of purple quartz crystals is made up of silicon-oxygen tetrahedra, linked to one another. This framework of tetrahedra is too complex to illustrate. The purple variety of quartz is called amethyst and its chemical composition is the same as pure quartz (SiO_2). However, there must be some difference to account for the difference in colour; pure quartz is colourless. The amethyst structure may contain some foreign atoms which cause the colour. The numbers of the foreign atoms are very small compared to the numbers of silicon and oxygen atoms, and there are not enough of them to affect the essential chemical composition, SiO_2.

Microcline, Another Framework Silicate (Plate 38)

Microcline belongs to the Feldspar Group of minerals, and it contains other atoms besides silicon and oxygen. This fine group, 15×20 centimetres in size, of triclinic microcline crystals exhibits a very pleasing green colour.

Some of the tetrahedra in microcline are made of silicon and oxygen atoms like the normal silicate unit; however, others are composed of aluminum and oxygen. The silicon atom and the aluminum atoms are similar in size and chemical nature and either one can be surrounded by four oxygen atoms in a tetrahedral arrangement. The characteristic part of the formula for microcline is $(AlSi_3O_8)$. Note that one aluminum atom plus three silicon atoms (together four atoms) are combined with eight oxygen atoms—one atom (either silicon or oxygen) to every two oxygens. The tetrahedral groups of atoms are arranged in a three-dimensional framework which has large "holes" in it. In the case of microcline, these "holes" are filled with potassium atoms (K) and the formula is $KAlSi_3O_8$. The crystal structure is too complex to draw properly and so a diagrammatic sketch is given in Fig. 8-10.

Some physical properties are: two perfect cleavage directions; hardness 6 to $6\frac{1}{2}$; specific gravity about 2.6; colour pink, green, white, yellow or red.

The other members of the Feldspar Group have similar structures, but different kinds of atoms are present in the large "holes" in the framework structure. These different atoms cause only slight changes in the physical properties of these minerals, so usually they are not easily distinguished from one another.

Scolecite, Another Framework Silicate (Plate 4)

Scolecite belongs to the Zeolite Group of minerals. It is a rather rare member of the group; but this specimen from Iceland is very attractive, being a radiating aggregate of delicate, colourless needles, the largest about six centimetres long.

The structures of the zeolite minerals have some similarities to the structures of the feldspars. The

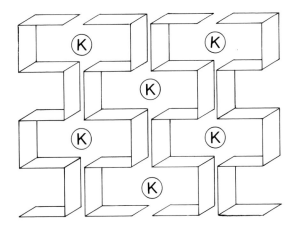

Fig 8-10 A basic feldspar structure. The zigzag chains represent fourfold rings of SiO tetrahedra as shown in the detailed sketch. Other atoms, like potassium, can occupy the large "holes" in the structure

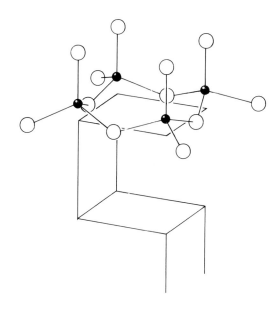

tetrahedral framework also contains large "holes"; some of them may be filled by other atoms and some by water molecules (H_2O).

The tetrahedra may be made of silicon and oxygen, or aluminum and oxygen. There are two aluminum atoms and three silicon atoms in the chemical formula of scolecite; so there must be ten oxygen atoms, two for each aluminum and two for each silicon. In addition, calcium atoms occupy some of the "holes" and water molecules occupy others. The full chemical formula is $Ca(Al_2Si_3O_{10}).3H_2O$.

There are many minerals in the Zeolite Group but each has the same basic framework structure. The differences lie in the kinds of atoms that occupy the "holes" in the framework.

Some physical properties of scolecite are: one perfect cleavage direction; hardness $5\frac{1}{2}$; specific gravity 2.2; colourless to white in colour, but may be yellow or red.

Some References

In the foregoing pages there are photographs, descriptions and principles relating to the science of mineralogy. It is hoped that the reader has not only gleaned some information about minerals but also been stimulated to think of some questions not answered here. If this is the case, this list of references will provide a source from which further knowledge may be obtained.

Bunn, C., *Crystals, Their Role in Nature and Science*, New York and London: Academic Press, 1964. Illustrated.

Dana, E. S. and Ford, W. E., *A Textbook of Mineralogy*, New York: John Wiley and Sons Inc., 1955. Illustrated.

de Michele, Vincenzo, *Il Mondo dei Cristalli*, Novara: Instituto Geografico de Agostini, I Documentari 7, 1967. Mainly colour photographs.

Desautels, P. E., *The Mineral Kingdom*, New York: Madison Square Press, 1969. Illustrated.

English, G. L. and Jensen, D. E., *Getting Acquainted with Minerals*, Revised Edition, New York: McGraw-Hill Book Co. Inc., 1958. Illustrated.

Holden, A. and Singer, P., *Crystals and Crystal Growing*, Garden City, New York: Doubleday and Co. Inc., 1960. Illustrated.

Hurlbut, C. S., *Dana's Manual of Mineralogy*, New York: John Wiley and Sons Inc., 1952. Illustrated.

Hurlbut, C. S., *Minerals and Man*, (The Worlds of Science Series), New York: Random House, 1968.

Gait, R. I., *The Gallery of Mineralogy — A Guide to the Teaching Section*, Toronto: Royal Ontario Museum, 1969. Illustrated.

Gait, R. I. and Meen, V. B., *The Gallery of Mineralogy — A General Guide*, Toronto: Royal Ontario Museum, 1969.

Sinkankas, J., *Mineralogy for Amateurs*, Princeton, New Jersey: D. Van Nostrand Company Inc., 1964. Illustrated. (Also published in Canada by Van Nostrand Company.)

Vanders, I. and Kerr, P. F., *Mineral Recognition*. New York: John Wiley and Sons Inc., 1967. Illustrated.

Index

Numbers in italics refer to illustrations

Agate, 46
Albite, 39
Almandine, 106
Alumino-silicates, 104
Aluminum, *10*, 28, 94, 104-105, 110, 114
Amazonite, *88*
Amethyst, 63, *88*, 113-114
Amphibole Group, 110-111
Ångstrom unit, 28-29, 67
Antimony, 93-94
Apatite, 70, *85*, 99-100
Apophyllite, *88*, 113
Argentite, 72
Arsenates, *see* Phosphates
Arsenic, 93-94
Arsenopyrite, 93
Asbestos, 45, 48
Aschynite, 49
Atom, 15, *17-18*, 27-*29*, *30-31*, *32-33*, *34-35*, 38, 51
Augite, *73*
Autunite, *86*, 100-101
Azurite, 47, 63

Barite, *23*, 55-56, *84*, 97, 99
Berman, Harry, 91
Beryl, 61, 103
Beryllium, 94
Betafite, *49*
Biotite, 75
Bismuth, 93-94
Borates, 97
Borax, 97
Bornite, 63
Bromine, 95

Calaverite, 93
Calcite, *22*, 57, 61, 63, 65, 70, *74*, *84*, 96-97
Calcium, 29, 55, 67, 99, 105, 110
Carbon, *23*, 35, *52*, 63, 67, 71, 73
Carbonates, 55, 96
Carborundum, 71
Carlsbad twins, *see* Orthoclase
Cassiterite, 48
Celestite, 97
Cerussite, 39-*40*, *95*
Chalcopyrite, *22*, 59
Chemical crystallography, *see* Mineralogy, subdivisions
Chlorine, 14, 95
Chromates, 99
Chrysoberyl, 94
Chrysotile, *44*-45
Chrysotile asbestos, 62
Clay, 62
Cleavage, 72-74

Colour, 63-64; spectrometer, 63; streak, 64
Compounds, 14, *17*, 29-30
Copper, 14, 28, 35, *44*-45, 54-55, 62, *72*, 75, 78, *85*, 96, 109
Corundum, 70-71
Crocoite, 99
Crystal aggregates, *19*, 42-46; botryoidal, *19*, 43, 45, 97; columnar, 45; dendritic, *44*-45; fibrous, *44*-45; foliated, 45; granular, 45; laminated, *20*, 45; oolitic, 45; pisolitic, 44; reniform, 45; stellated, *19*, 42
Chrystal chemistry, *see* Mineralogy, subdivisions; also *34*-35
Crystals: growth of, 51-59; impure, *55*-56; overgrowths, *22*, 59; partial phantom, *22*, 54-55, 57; phantom, *22*, 53-55; sceptre, *58*-59; single, 37-38; skeletal, *59;* systems, 32; twisted, *57*-59; *see also* Calcite, Gypsum, Twin crystals
Cyclosilicates, *86*, *107-108*-109

Dana, James Dwight (Dana System of Classification), 91-92
Descloisite, 100-101
Diamagnetic, *see* Mineral properties, magnetic
Diamond, 14-15, *31*, 35, *52*-53, 61-63, 67, 70-72, 74, *82*, 93
Diopside, 110
Dioptase, *86*, 109
Dolomite, *19*, 39, 48, 55, 97

Economic geology, *see* Geology, subdivisions
Elements, 14-15, 27
Enstatite, 110
Epidote, 107
Erythrite, 100

Feldspar, *115*
Feldspar Group, 104, 113-114
Fergusonite, 49
Ferromagnetic, *see* Mineral properties, magnetic
Fluorescence, 64-65
Fluorine, 48, 67, 95
Fluorite, *24*, 39-*40*, 63, 65-66, 70, 74, *84*, 95-96
Fracture, 74-75; conchoidal, 74-75, *76;* hackly, 75; splintery, 75
Frondel, Clifford, 91

Galena, *14*-15, *17-18*, 29-30, 33, 59, 62, 73-*74*, 93, 95
Garnet, 71, 103
Garnet Group, *86*, 105-106
Geology, 11; subdivisions, 11
Geophysics, *see* Geology, subdivisions
Goethite, 94
Gold, 14, *23*, 28, 67, 72, 75, 78, *82*, 93-94
Graphite, 15, 45, *52*-53, 63, 67, 71, 73
Grossular, *86*, 105-106
Gypsum, *39-40*, 61-62, 70, 72, 97-*98*-99; rosette, *85*

Halides, 95-96
Halite, 14, 52, 73-74, *84*, 95
Hardness, 69-72; hardness points, *70*
Haüy, the Abbé, 38
Heavy liquids, 67
Hematite, 45, 55, 75, 77-*78*, *83*, 94-*95*
Hornblende, 63, 73, *88*, 103, 110-111
Hydromagnesite, 96
Hydroxides, *see* Oxides

Ilmenite, 94
Inclusions in crystals, *56*-57, 63
Inosilicates, *88*, *110-111*
Iodine, 95
Iron, 28, 56, 64, 77-78, 94, 105, 110
Kaolin, 62
Kimberlite, *53*
Kyanite, *24*, 71

Law of constant interfacial angles, 38
Lead, 29-30
Lechatelierite, 48
Lustre, adamantine, earthy, greasy, pearly, resinous, silky, vitreous, waxy, 62-63

Magnesium, 105, 110
Magnetite, 75-78
Malachite, *19*, 45-46, 63, 97
Manganese, 63, 65
Mercury, 14
Metamict minerals, 48-*49*, 79
Meteorite, *12-13*
Mica, 73
Mica Group, 15, 45, 72-73, 103
Microline, *88*, 114-*115*
Mineral, definition of, 13-14
Mineralogy, definition, 11; subdivisions, 13
Mineral properties: electrical, 77-78; magnetic, 75, 78; optical 79; radioactive, 79
Mohs Hardness Scale, *70*
Molybdates, 101
Molybdenite, 63
Morphological crystallography, *see* Mineralogy, subdivisions
Muscovite, *20*, 45, 72, 104, 111

Native elements, *81-82*, 92-93
Natural glasses, 48
Nepheline, 62
Nesosilicates, *86*, *104-105*-106
Nickel, 77
Nitrates, 97
Nitre, 97
Non-crystalline minerals: glasses, 48; metamict, 48-49

Olivine, 45
Olivine Group, 105
Optical crystallography, *see* Mineralogy, subdivisions
Orpiment, 73
Orthoclase, 39, 46, *48*, 70
Orthosilicate Group, 108
Overgrowths, *see* Crystals
Oxides, 94-96

Palache, Charles, 91
Palaeontology, *see* Geology, subdivisions
Paramagnetic, *see* Mineral properties, magnetic
Petrified wood, *21*, 46
Petrology, *see* Geology, subdivisions
Phosphates, 99-100
Phosphorescence, 65
Phyllosilicates, *20*, *88*, *111-112-*113
Physical mineralogy, *see* Mineralogy, subdivisions
Physical mixture, 29
Piezoelectricity, *see* Mineral properties, electrical
Plagioclase, *41*
Plagioclase Group, 39
Potassium, 29, 110, 114
Priorite, 49
Proustite, 94
Pseudomorphs, 46-47
Pyrite, 30, 62, *83*, 93-94
Pyroelectricity, *see* Mineral properties, electrical
Pyrope, 106
Pyroxene Group, 73, 110-111

Pyrrhotite, 75

Quartz, *22*, *24*, 46, 48, 56, *58*, 61-64, 70, 72, 75-*76*, 78, 103, 109, 113

Salt, *see* Halite
Scheelite, 101
Scolecite, *19*, 42, 114-115
Selenium, 93
Serpentine, 62
Silicates, 103-115
Silicon-oxygen framework, *see* Tektosilicates
Silicon-oxygen tetrahedron, 103-*104-105*
Silver, 28, 35, 62, 75, 78
Sodium, 14, 110
Sorosilicates, *87*, *106*-108
Specific gravity, 65-67
Sperrylite, 93
Sphalerite, *22*, 56, 59, 63-64, 74, *82*, 93
Steno, Nicolaus, 38
Stratigraphy, *see* Geology, subdivisions
Strontium, 29
Structural crystallography, *see* Mineralogy, subdivisions
Sulphates, 97, 99
Sulphides, 93-94
Sulphosalts, 94
Sulphur, *22*, 28-29, *55*-56, 59, 63, *82*, 93
Symmetry, *31*, 33-34, 37-38

Talc, 45, 70-73
Tektosilicates, *19*, *88*, 113-115
Tellurium, 93
Tenacity, 72

Tetrahedra: chains of, *see* Inosilicates; double, *see* Sorosilicates; independent, *see* Nesosilicates; rings of, *see* Cyclosilicates; sheets of, *see* Phyllosilicates
Thorite, 79
Thorium, 79
Tiger eye, *47*-48
Tin, 94
Titanium, 63, 94
Topaz, 48, 62, 70, 73, 103
Tourmaline, 78
Tourmaline Group, 103
Transparency, 61
Triphylite, 99
Tungstates, *see* Molybdates
Twin crystals, 39-40, *84*, 96; "butterfly," *40;* cyclic, 39-*40;* interpenetration, *19*, 39-*40;* "swallowtail," *39*

Ultraviolet (UV) light, 64-65
Uraninite, *24*, 66-67, 79, 94
Uranium, 65, 67, 79
Uvarovite, 106

Vanadates, *see* Phosphates
Vanadinite, *85*, 100

Wavellite, *42*
Wulfenite, *86*, 101

Zeolite Group, 104, 114-115
Zinc, *55*-56, 59, 64
Zoisite, *87*, 107-108